Person and Character Level Life Coaching and Mentoring **Training and Practice Resources**

Life Coaching and Mentoring from an Expanded Paradigm

Dr. Dennis Morgan

Person and Character Level Life Coaching and Mentoring Training and Practice Resources
by Dr. Dennis Morgan. Copyright © 2018 by Dr. Dennis Morgan. All rights reserved.
ISBN: 978-0-9982118-3-1
Graphics & Layout: OM EAST, Spillern, Austria.
Bible quotations are from the English Standard Version.
Dr. Morgan can be contacted at: personlifecoach@gmail.com

Table of Contents

FORMS

TOOLS

WORKSHEETS

ENDNOTES

REFERENCES

Preface

This Training and Practice Resources (TPR) book has been developed as a companion to *Person and Character Level Life Coaching and Mentoring*.[1] It is intended to provide Life Mentors and Life Coaches with resources related to their training. As well, there are additional resources that are useful for the ongoing practice of this *Person and Character Level* model of Life Mentoring and Coaching.

The structural *Person and Character Level* (PCL) model or paradigm, with the immaterial soul as the person, need not be viewed as simplistic. All the biblical redemptive realities apply, especially the divine and permanent re-creative act of regeneration. As well, those concerned with an appreciation of the complexities of the human psyche can rest assured that there is no limit placed upon psychological understandings or processes, but rather what is offered is a grounded perspective that this psychological functioning is rightfully attributed to the material brain. With both the immaterial and material aspects of the individual accounted for, there is also a commitment to maintaining the reality of there being an integrated whole person.

The PCL model provides an underlying structure for understanding the person and change. The model is being used here to provide this structure for PCL Life Mentoring and Life Coaching modalities, but the same foundational structure for assisting in the change process can be considered for counseling and psychotherapy modalities as well. The boundary around the modality used with clients is established by the choice of goals and interventions. The PCL Life Mentoring and Life Coaching goals and interventions are distinguished and set apart from the psychological goals and interventions that would characterize counseling and psychotherapy. Thus, the PCL model in this set of Training and Practice Resources is oriented, through goals and interventions, to fit with life mentoring and coaching.

Regarding the organization of this book, the first part of the material is a combination of in-class lecture notes for the two separate but integrated PCL Life Mentoring and Life Coaching trainings. The PCL Life Mentor training lecture notes are first, because they present the beginning or entry level of training. The PCL Life Coaching lecture notes are the second half and complete the in-class material. As will be seen, lecture notes are designed with blanks to fill in and corresponding content found in the footnotes. As participants listen to the lectures, they are to be actively writing the content in the blanks. This is intended as a way to keep participants actively engaged and to reinforce their learning. As well, participants will leave the trainings with a completed set of notes that can be reviewed later.

The second part of this set of Training and Practice Resources is composed of appendices that are divided into categories. The Diagram appendices include the flow charts and the whole person illustration. The Further Explanations section contains appendices related to the soul-person concept of identity reorienting that occurs in PCL Life Mentoring and Coaching. The next part of the appendices includes useful forms for recording the different aspects of meetings with clients and for keeping track of practice hours. The Tools set of appendices includes practical resources that are summary reminders and guidelines to use when doing PCL Life Mentoring and Coaching practice and supervision. The final category of the appendices includes the PCL Life Mentoring worksheets — both the Consciously-Christian client version and the revised worksheets for the Not-Consciously-Christian clients.

While using the material in this resource book, it will become evident that PCL Life Mentoring and PCL Life Coaching are an integrated whole. PCL Life Mentoring is a valuable means for offering support, but it is not the end state for training. PCL Life Coaching is the full preparation for a person and character level approach to helping others make positive changes in their lives from the depth of the soul-person.

PERSON AND CHARACTER LEVEL (PCL) TRAINING DAYS

PCL LIFE MENTORING TRAINING DAY AGENDA AND NOTES

PCL Life Mentoring Training Day Agenda – **Example**

8:30	Gathering and Greeting
9:00	**I. Foundations in PCL Life Mentoring**
10:15	Break
10:30	**I. Foundations in PCL Life Mentoring** (continued)
12:00	Lunch
13:00	**II. In-Class PCL Life Mentoring Structured Practice**
14:00	Break
14:15	**II. In-Class PCL Life Mentoring Structured Practice** (continued)
15:15	Break
15:30	**III. Post-Class PCL Life Mentoring Structured and Supervised Practice**
16:00	Ending Time

Training Objectives

1. Participants will learn key foundational spiritual and personal factors for intentionally helping others toward positive change.

2. Participants will be given information on use of key spiritual and personal change factors.

3. Participants will become familiar with the Life Mentoring model of change.

4. Participants will understand how to conduct a Life Mentoring meeting using the *Life in Process* Worksheets.

Materials for the Training

- Copy of PCL Life Mentoring Training Day Agenda (provided)

- Dr. Morgan's combined life mentoring and life coaching materials in ***Person and Character Level Life Coaching and Mentoring*** book (as provided or available from Amazon).

- Dr. Morgan's ***Person and Character Level Life Coaching and Mentoring Training and Practice Resources*** book (as provided or available from Amazon).

I. Foundations in PCL Life Mentoring

1. Person and Character Level (PCL) Life Mentoring and Coaching provide a

   _____ for effectively
   helping others to change — personal change, both internally and externally.[1]

2. In PCL Life Mentoring and Coaching, it is important to identify:

   2.1. What _____ are you wanting to accomplish?[2]

   2.2. Whose _____ are these?[3]

   2.3. What _____ need to be taken to reach
   these goals?[4]

3. PCL Life Coaching training is the second of two levels of training:

   _____.[5]

4. The PCL Life Mentoring level is structured, but the second level, Life Coaching,
   is not as structured an approach for helping, though both follow the same

   _____.[6]

5. The PCL Life Mentoring and separate PCL Life Coaching flow chart diagrams
   (see Appendices A and B) give a brief description of the process-for-change
   that also allows

   _____ to be fit into the

   _____ (e.g., programs
   such as GriefShare[II]).[7]

---

[1]   1. general model
[2]   2.1. changes
[3]   2.2. goals
[4]   2.3. actions
[5]   3. Life Mentoring and Life Coaching
[6]   4. process/stages of change
[7]   5. specific content   general model

6. PCL Life Coaching, like PCL Life Mentoring is focused on the

   _____ and not on
   the person's past/there and then (except to provide relevant information to
   understand responses to the current situation).[8]

7. In PCL Life Coaching, as in PCL Life Mentoring, there are *3 Core Realities*
   to understand:

   7.1. Change happens through _____.[9]

   7.2. Humans are whole persons, but also are both

        _____ , and
        Life Mentoring and Life Coaching help the real person (the spiritual
        part, the soul-person) to learn how to manage the whole person.[10]

   7.3. The foundation for personal change is based in the

        _____ (functioning virtues) of the person.[11]

8. In both PCL Life Mentoring and Life Coaching there are *3 Central
   Principles* to keep working on with clients.

   8.1. Staying in the _____ and addressing the

        _____.[12]

   8.2. Staying connected in the _____ with

        _____.[13]

---

[8]   6. present/here and now
[9]   7.1. relationships
[10] 7.2. physical and spiritual beings
[11] 7.3. character
[12] 8.1. present   current situation
[13] 8.2. present   God or a higher power

8.3. Developing _____ :
identifying what virtues, if present or present more strongly and then
practiced, would improve the person's management of the situation.[14]

9. PCL Life Mentors and Coaches keep the related *3 Life Goals* in mind at all times:

9.1. Strengthening the _____
with God or the higher power.[15]

9.2. Increasing _____
and/or Christlikeness.[16]

9.3. Improving _____.[17]

10. In the PCL Life Mentoring and Coaching process for helping another, there
are *3 Stages of Change*:

10.1. Telling the _____.[18]

10.2. Setting _____.[19]

10.3. Taking _____.[20]

11. PCL Life Mentors and Coaches help others, in

_____, to deal with
and make changes in their current situation, while not neglecting the

_____ in the here and
now relating with God or a higher power and growth in relevant virtues.[21]

---

[14] 8.3. character strength
[15] 9.1. here and now relationship
[16] 9.2. character virtues
[17] 9.3. coping and resilience
[18] 10.1. Story
[19] 10.2. Situational Goals
[20] 10.3. Action
[21] 11. practical ways   spiritual change

12. PCL Life Mentoring and Life Coaching are addressing a

_____ ,

but are not focused on counseling or psychotherapy goals, and they may at times incorporate specific instruction (teaching) on topics related to spiritual and personal growth.[22]

13. PCL Mentoring and Life Coaching can be with individuals who self-identify as Christians, as well as those who don't — the

_____ ,

because they share much in _____ .[23]

    13.1. Both are created in the _____
         (in the book of Genesis sense).[24]

    13.2. Both have the same _____
         of being both physical and spiritual, but within a whole person.[25]

    13.3. Both are able to change from the _____

         person and character _____
         into the brain and body functioning.[26]

14. There are also important distinctions when working with those who are Consciously-Christian:

    14.1. Regeneration of the spiritual: the soul person with a

    _____ .[27]

---

[22]   12. deeper level of change
[23]   13. Not-Consciously-Christian   common
[24]   13.1. image of God
[25]   13.2. human nature structure
[26]   13.3. inside   outward
[27]   14.1. new nature

14.2. Freedom from the _____.[28]

14.3. Empowerment from the indwelling _____.[29]

15. There are additional important concepts and implications to consider in both PCL Life Mentoring and Life Coaching:

15.1. _____.[30]

15.2. _____.[31]

15.3. Change in the context of _____.[32]

15.4. _____ implications for change.[33]

15.5. _____.[34]

Human Nature

16. Human beings are composed of two substances:

_____.[35]

17. The immaterial substance is referred to as the

_____.[36]

18. The material substance is the

_____.[37]

---

[28] 14.2. power of sin
[29] 14.3. Holy Spirit
[30] 15.1. Human Nature
[31] 15.2. Virtues
[32] 15.3. relationship
[33] 15.4. Self-efficacy
[34] 15.5. Resilience
[35] 16. immaterial and material
[36] 17. soul or spirit
[37] 18. brain and body

19. _____ asserts that there is a
nonmaterial aspect to a person, a soul, and that there is a material brain and
a material body, with the nonmaterial and material working together as a

_____ (see Appendix C).[38]

20. Mankind can only have _____
that is either the old sinful nature or the new regenerate nature of the soul
or spirit.[39]

21. Having been given a new or recreated nature in regeneration, however, does
not eliminate all the effects of having been fallen, because

_____ remain in the

_____.[40]

22. The believer's struggle is understood to be between the

_____ (soul/spirit)

and the _____ (in the brain and body),
with the person being empowered the Holy Spirit.[41]

23. The believer approaches the struggle by acknowledging that, "I am the

_____ enabled to defeat

the _____
remaining imperfections".[42]

---

[38]   19. Holistic dualism   unified whole
[39]   20. one nature
[40]   21. sinful dispositions   brain and body
[41]   22. person   flesh
[42]   23. new person   non-person

Virtues

24. Character is here believed to be the functioning of the

_____

within the person (see Appendix N).[43]

25. _____ change
is about personality functioning changing, but when focused on the

_____ changing, then something
is changing regarding human nature and virtues or character.[44]

Relationship

26. Much work can be done applying principles, such as those in *Life in Process*

worksheets, but what is experienced in _____
with the mentor and ultimately with God is at the heart of change[III].[45]

27. Life Mentoring holds that the unfolding of relationship is more important
than techniques, and that the life mentor-offered

_____ are the most
important factor for influencing change in clients.[46]

[43] 24. composite of virtues
[44] 25. Psychological   person
[45] 26. relationship
[46] 27. relationship conditions

Self-Efficacy

28. Self-efficacy means that the person's

_____ ,
concerning oneself and resources, are indicating having confidence in the

_____ oneself.[47]

29. There is more empowerment of self-efficacy when it is understood that one's

person is _____ from one's brain and body,

and the person can make _____ to effect change
in the brain and body.[48]

30. _____ and personal issues can then be viewed
from the perspective of not being the deepest desires of the person, but

rather the functioning of the _____.[49]

31. With the inner sense of _____
from brain/body problematic functioning, the person can then more readily
and effectively address these problems of sin and dysfunction.[50]

32. The effects of regeneration, justification, and sanctification should be

understood as providing a _____
who is enabled by the Holy Spirit to influence the brain and body, thus
directing the whole person to being more consistently Christ-like.[51]

---

[47]   28. beliefs and actions   ability to change
[48]   29. distinct   choices
[49]   30. Sin   brain and body
[50]   31. detachment
[51]   32. solid new person

33. Seeing oneself in this manner both grounds and increases _____
    — a hope that one can experience change and in fact will be changed.[52]

34. Granted that unbelievers have not been freed from the power of sin, but
    even so, when unbelievers are able to affirm having an

    _____ they are enabled to
    identify more readily with an ability to make choices over internal processes
    and external behaviors of the material part.[53]

35. Believers, having a clear understanding that their _____
    as distinct from their brain and body functioning, are enabled potentially to

    an even greater extent to enact the _____
    that can be made, because of also being freed from the power of sin and
    empowered by the Holy Spirit.[54]

Resilience[IV]

36. A qualitative change toward a deeper _____

    to God and strengthened _____
    are here promoted as the primary underlying means for coping with,
    managing, and transcending life challenges and related personal issues.[55]

37. The mentor's _____
    is to promote the strengthening of the person's intimate bond with God and
    character virtues.[56]

---

[52]   33. hope
[53]   34. immaterial person
[54]   35. persons   choices
[55]   36. connection   character
[56]   37. ultimate goal

38. When the quality of one's real-time relationship with God is improved and the person's character more developed, then the

    _____ life challenges and suffering is strengthened and established.[57]

39. The increased sense of God's closeness and personal involvement, along with increased self-understanding, character, and conscious or willed change in

    functioning, increases one's _____ to the circumstances of life.[58]

---

[57] 38. ability to transcend
[58] 39. resilience

II. In-Class PCL Life Mentoring Structured Practice

1. The design of the PCL Life Mentor training includes

   _____ practice, within the use of the *Life in Process*[V] Worksheets (see Appendix L).[59]

2. The in-class portion of the PCL Life Mentor training includes

   _____ ,
   while using the *Life in Process* Worksheets (see Appendices O and P).[60]

3. PCL Life Mentor training teaches people how to come along side of others in a helpfully structured

   _____ manner.[61]

4. PCL Life Mentor training practice temporarily restricts the way of helping others, to the use of the *Life in Process* worksheets, which:

   4.1. Reduces the _____ of being responsible to direct an unstructured conversation.[62]

   4.2. Takes the individual life mentoring meetings through the

   _____ process within individual meetings, as well as across all the meetings.[63]

   4.3. Allows the life mentor trainee to take

   _____ for keeping the focus of the meeting on how to go through the *Stages of Change*, cover *Central Principles*, and include the *Life Goals*.[64]

---

[59]　1. skill-building
[60]　2. practice with another participant
[61]　3. intentional and personal
[62]　4.1. stress
[63]　4.2. *3 Stages of Change*
[64]　4.3. less responsibility

4.4. At the same time, the worksheets are structured to bring out the

_____ ,

instead of imposing the trainee's agenda.[65]

4.5. The *Life in Process* worksheets _____
more clearly with the stages of change: Story, Goals, and Action.[66]

5. PCL Life Mentor trainees need to become comfortable with the

_____

and not just with using specific approaches such as:[67]

5.1. Teaching Bible content.

5.2. Imparting advice.

5.3. Using spiritual interventions, such as intercessory prayer.

5.4. Stressing accountability.

---

[65]   4.4. client's story
[66]   4.5. correspond
[67]   5. process of change

III. *Post-Class PCL Life Mentoring Structured and Supervised Practice*

1. PCL Life Mentor training in its entirety is more than the in-class time and

   requires a time of _____
   with a practice client, in order to become skilled in and not just familiar with
   the principles of life mentoring.[68]

2. The post-class follow-ups, to build skill competence in life mentoring, include the

   _____

   and the ongoing group and/or individual

   _____

   (separate from the life mentoring practice sessions), where trainees talk about
   the life mentoring sessions they are having with their clients (see Appendix M).[69]

3. A certificate is earned after _____ of

   life mentoring practice with a client and _____ of
   supervision time (see Appendix J).[70]

4. Subsequent to participating in the Life Mentor Training, individuals are
   ready for the in-class

   _____ ,

   with its own post-class supervised practice.[71]

5. After completing the supervised practice of an additional _____

   of meetings with clients and _____ of
   group supervision, the Life Coaching Certificate is earned.[72]

---

[68] 1. supervised practice
[69] 2. life mentoring practice sessions   supervision meetings
[70] 3. 50 hours   25 hours
[71] 4. Life Coaching Training
[72] 5. 50 hours   25 hours

6. The most significant learning, about how to be a PCL Life Mentor, occurs

during the _____ practice[73]

---

[73]   6. supervised

PCL LIFE COACHING TRAINING DAY AGENDA AND NOTES

PCL Life Coaching Training Day Agenda – Example

8:30	Gathering and Greeting
9:00	**I. Reinforcing the Foundation**
10:15	Break
10:30	**II. A Soul-Person Concept of Identity: The Impact of Owning Who I am**
12:00	Lunch
13:00	**III. The Ten Tasks and the Life Coaching Basics**
14:00	Break
14:15	**IV. Using the Ten Tasks with the Soul-Person Concept of Identity**
15:15	Break
15:30	**V. The PCL Life Coaching Supervised Practice Experience**
16:00	Ending Time

Training Objectives

1. Participants will gain a clarified understanding of the process that is happening in intentional, supportive interpersonal interactions.

2. Participants will obtain further information regarding changes to the client's concept of identity.

3. Participants will become familiar with the *Ten Tasks* model.

4. Participants will understand how to use the *Ten Tasks* model to effectively encourage change in others.

Materials for the Training

- Copy of PCL Life Coaching Training Day Agenda (provided)

- Dr. Morgan's combined life mentoring and life coaching materials in ***Person and Character Level Life Coaching and Mentoring*** book (as provided or available from Amazon).

- Dr. Morgan's ***Person and Character Level Life Coaching and Mentoring Training and Practice Resources*** book (as provided or available from Amazon).

I. Reinforcing the Foundation

1. Person and Character Level (PCL) Life Mentoring and Coaching provide a

   _____ for effectively helping others to change – personal change, both internally and externally.[74]

2. In PCL Life Mentoring and Coaching, it is important to identify:

   2.1. What _____ are you wanting to accomplish?[75]

   2.2. Whose _____ are these?[76]

   2.3. What _____ need to be taken to reach these goals?[77]

3. PCL Life Coaching training is the second of two levels of training:

   _____.[78]

4. The PCL Life Mentoring level is structured, but the second level, Life Coaching, is not as structured an approach for helping, though both follow the same

   _____.[79]

5. The PCL Life Mentoring and separate PCL Life Coaching flow chart diagrams (see Appendices A and B) give a brief description of the process-for-change that also allows

   _____ to be fit into the

   _____ (e.g., programs such as GriefShare[VI]).[80]

---

[74] 1. general model
[75] 2.1. changes
[76] 2.2. goals
[77] 2.3. actions
[78] 3. Life Mentoring and Life Coaching
[79] 4. process/stages of change
[80] 5. specific content   general model

6. PCL Life Coaching, like PCL Life Mentoring is focused on the

   _____ and not on the person's past/there and then (except to provide relevant information to understand responses to the current situation).[81]

7. In PCL Life Coaching, as in PCL Life Mentoring, there are *3 Core Realities* to understand:

   7.1. Change happens through _____.[82]

   7.2. Humans are whole persons, but also are both

      _____,

      and Life Coaching helps the real person (the spiritual part, the soul-person) to learn how to manage the whole person.[83]

   7.3. The foundation for personal change is based in the

      _____ (functioning virtues) of the person.[84]

8. In both PCL Life Mentoring and Life Coaching there are *3 Central Principles* to keep working on with clients.

   8.1. Staying in the _____ and

      addressing the _____.[85]

   8.2. Staying connected in the _____ with

      _____.[86]

---

[81] 6. present/here and now
[82] 7.1. relationships
[83] 7.2. physical and spiritual beings
[84] 7.3. character
[85] 8.1. present   current situation
[86] 8.2. present   God or a higher power

8.3. Developing _____:
identifying what virtues, if present or present more strongly and then practiced, would improve the person's management of the situation.[87]

9. PCL Life Mentors and Coaches keep the related *3 Life Goals* in mind at all times:

9.1. Strengthening the _____ with God or the higher power.[88]

9.2. Increasing _____ and/or Christlikeness.[89]

9.3. Improving _____.[90]

10. In the PCL Life Mentoring and Coaching process for helping another, there are *3 Stages of Change*:

10.1. Telling the _____.[91]

10.2. Setting _____.[92]

10.3. Taking _____.[93]

11. PCL Life Mentors and Coaches help others, in

_____, to deal with and make changes in their current situation, while not neglecting the

_____ in here and now relating with God or a higher power and growth in relevant virtues.[94]

---

[87] 8.3. character strength
[88] 9.1. here and now relationship
[89] 9.2. character virtues
[90] 9.3. coping and resilience
[91] 10.1. Story
[92] 10.2. Situational Goals
[93] 10.3. Action
[94] 11. practical ways   spiritual change

12. PCL Life Mentoring and Life Coaching are addressing a

    _____,
    but are not focused on counseling or psychotherapy goals, and they may at
    times incorporate specific instruction (teaching) on topics related to spiritual
    and personal growth.[95]

13. PCL Mentoring and Life Coaching can be with individuals who self-identify
    as Christians, as well as those who don't — the

    _____,

    because they share much in _____.[96]

    13.1. Both are created in the _____
          (in the book of Genesis sense).[97]

    13.2. Both have the same _____
          of being both physical and spiritual, but within a whole person.[98]

    13.3. Both are able to change from the _____

          person and character _____
          into the brain and body functioning.[99]

14. There are also important distinctions when working with those who are
    Consciously-Christian:

    14.1. Regeneration of the spiritual: the soul person with a

    _____.[100]

_____

[95]   12. deeper level of change
[96]   13. Not-Consciously-Christian   common
[97]   13.1. image of God
[98]   13.2. human nature structure
[99]   13.3. inside   outward
[100] 14.1. new nature

14.2. Freedom from the _____.[101]

14.3. Empowerment from the indwelling _____.[102]

15. There are additional important concepts and implications to consider in both PCL Life Mentoring and Life Coaching:

15.1. _____.[103]

15.2. _____.[104]

15.3. Change in the context of _____.[105]

15.4. _____ implications for change.[106]

15.5. _____.[107]

---

[101] 14.2. power of sin
[102] 14.3. Holy Spirit
[103] 15.1. Human Nature
[104] 15.2. Virtues
[105] 15.3. relationship
[106] 15.4. Self-efficacy
[107] 15.5. Resiliency

II. A Soul-Person Concept of Identity: The Impact of Owning Who I am

1. In *Person and Character Level Life Coaching* (PCL) intentional change occurs, and this can include a modification to one's personal

   _____

   (see Appendix D).[108]

2. In other words, during the PCL Life Coaching process, clients will likely become increasingly aware of their self-concept and that changes are happening – that their concept of identity is

   _____.[109]

3. This reorienting is grounded in their _____ being

   defined as their _____, and other aspects of their concept of identity are then derived from and/or are congruent with this foundational reality.[110]

4. This reorienting of clients' concepts of identity will likely be a

   _____ of the PCL Life Coaching process.[111]

5. It is therefore important to provide PCL Life Coaches with more extensive information, so that they: can have a

   _____ of identity concepts and of the soul-person concept of identity in particular, can more

   _____ this identity concept to their clients, and are better able to

   _____ of their clients' concepts of identity.[112]

---

[108]   1. self-concept or concept of identity
[109]   2. reorienting
[110]   3. soul   real person
[111]   4. natural part
[112]   5. fuller understanding   clearly explain   assist the reorienting

6. We go about our daily lives performing a multitude of actions, but who initiates them? We are quick to say I do them and I initiate them. This

   _____ is who we identify as _____,
   the concept we have of who we are — our

   _____.[113]

7. One's concept of identity is related to

   _____

   and comes into play in order to adequately and successfully face these external and internal challenges of life.[114]

8. PCL Life Coaching is an _____,
   with a process and goals to enhance this coping and resilience, but from a

   perspective that also utilizes an _____
   of personal identity.[115]

9. The concept of one's identity is _____

   self or person, it is rather _____
   one is and then functions in life accordingly.[116]

10. As can be imagined, this identity concept can both

    _____ what one believes
    is possible when faced with normal everyday life, as well as with the exceptional challenges of life.[117]

---

[113] 6. "I"   our person   self-concept
[114] 7. how we do things
[115] 8. intentional relationship   expanded concept
[116] 9. not the actual   who one thinks
[117] 10. expand and limit

11. It is crucial that one's concept of identity be not only _____,

but also _____ and account for all of who the person is. In particular, all the primary dimensions of human existence need to be accounted for.[118]

12. In PCL Life Coaching, human beings are understood to be more than and distinct from their material brain and body processes.

The _____ as well as the

_____ dimensions must both be included in the concept of one's identity.[119]

13. In PCL Life Coaching there is an addressing of the reality that there is a spiritual,

_____ to the person's identity.[120]

14. The addition of this spiritual reality, to one's concept of identity, is given

definite form because the _____ is explained to be the location of the person, not the physical brain (see Appendix C).

This _____ interacts with, but also has functions beyond and above the brain and body.[121]

15. Defining the soul as being the person and then understanding that it is the

_____ who _____ the brain and can effectively influence the brain, contributes positively to a change in clients' concepts of their personal identities.[122]

---

[118] 11. accurate   thorough
[119] 12. immaterial   material
[120] 13. immaterial dimension
[121] 14. immaterial soul   immaterial person
[122] 15. soul-person   animates

16. It will be new to clients and perhaps feel foreign to have this reoriented

    concept of their _____.[123]

17. This concept of identity shift, however, has greater potential for

    _____ one's whole person — someone inside one's

    whole self who can effectively _____
    from problems and problematic internal psychological processes and make

    _____ and prompt _____
    that moves the brain and body in healthy directions.[124]

18. _____ teaching about
    the soul-person identity concept occurs within the PCL Life Coaching Ten
    Tasks process (also see Appendix F).[125]

19. The PCL Life Coach can _____ mention
    to clients the importance of the concept of identity and how that identity

    concept can be _____ in the reality of

    their being an immaterial _____.[126]

20. Bergner and Holmes state that the self-concept (or one's concept of identity)
    is most usefully defined as a summary of one's

    _____ to the rest of the world,

    including oneself — for example the _____
    of one's own self-worth. [127]

---

[123] 16. identity as a soul-person
[124] 17. managing   self-distance   choices   action
[125] 18. Direct and indirect
[126] 19. directly   grounded   soul-person
[127] 20. position in relation   evaluation

21. Bergner and Holmes recommend helping clients change their self-concepts

    by relating to them in ways _____

    with their self-concepts, thus indirectly _____
    to the person a different self-concept.[128]

22. This is a kind of self-concept _____
    change — a higher status self-concept than had been the client's.[129]

23. In PCL Life Coaching, clients' self-concepts or identity statuses are further

    _____ by their learning that

    they are an immaterial _____
    to whom these higher statuses are assigned.[130]

24. It is the _____
    that is offered to clients as the basis for personal identity. This soul-person
    identity concept includes the idea that the client has the potential to

    _____ these statuses.[131]

25. One can see the definite advantage, of the PCL Life Coaching understanding

    of human nature, because the soul-person is _____
    from the brain and body — being of a different substance, so able to have a

    _____ vantage point from
    which to own the soul-person concept of identity and from which to

    _____ the brain and body.[132]

---

[128] 21. incompatible   communicating
[129] 22. status
[130] 23. reinforced   soul-person
[131] 24. soul-person identity concept   actualize
[132] 25. distinct   self-distanced   act upon

26. The facilitating of a new identity concept can be communicated through the

    indirect relational _____ (e.g., congruence, positive regard, and empathy).[133]

27. The direct education approach would include: providing _____ about the soul-person concept of identity and the change process, making

    personal _____ to the client, and in general to

    continue to _____ PCL Life Coaching related concepts. The two approaches can and likely will occur together — through the indirect PCL Life Coaching attitudes and by directly educating.[134]

28. This soul-person _____,
    along with the personal acknowledgment that the soul-person is the

    _____, can be nurtured in

    clients. They can then better _____ the abilities that their soul-persons have been given and can be open to the

    continuous _____ of their soul-persons.[135]

29. To own my soul-person identity as my concept of who I am and to build

    upon it, is an opportunity to live _____

    with the original human design, to be _____

    by self-concept, and to be _____ to flourish.[136]

---

[133] 26. attitudes
[134] 27. information   applications   reinforce
[135] 28. concept of identity   true identity   utilize   development
[136] 29. congruently   unhindered   freed

III. The Ten Tasks and the Life Coaching Basics

1. The *Ten Tasks* is the name given to a list of PCL Life Coaching _____

   or _____ that the PCL Life Coach _____

   _____ and _____

   during life coaching meetings.[137]

2. The principle of actively listening to the client's *story* is in the

   _____ of the life coaching
   process, in which the life coach attempts to fully understand the client's
   situational events, reactions, and relevant background (the story of the
   client's life).[138]

3. While listening and interacting with the client, the PCL Life Coach does this

   with certain *attitudes*: _____

   _____.[139]

   3.1. Congruence means that life coaches are concerned to allow clients to

   experience them _____ — the
   life coach's internal and external experiences are one and the same.[140]

   3.2. Positive regard refers to the life coach's deep and

   _____ for the client

   — showing _____
   toward the client's person.[141]

---

[137] 1. Basics   principles   pays attention to   does
[138] 2. first stage
[139] 3. Congruence, Positive Regard, and Empathy
[140] 3.1. authentically
[141] 3.2. genuine caring   acceptance

3.3. Empathy is the ability to understand what the client is feeling — to

understand _____

the client's _____
in the here-and-now.[142]

4. Setting ***situational goals*** is in the _____
of the PCL Life Coaching process.[143]

4.1. Situational goals are _____
goals that will emerge from the client's story.[144]

4.2. For example, a situational goal would be for a client to resolve a

_____ with a friend.[145]

5. Identifying client shifting parts or ***modes*** is for the life coach's benefit to be

able to understand surprising _____

and _____.[146]

5.1. There are potentially dysfunctional _____,

dysfunctional _____,

and dysfunctional _____
modes in clients that negatively influence their moods and reactions.[147]

5.2. The PCL Life Coach sometimes _____
mode reactions that are in their clients, in order to give clients a
chance to make good choices.[148]

---

[142] 3.3. sensitively and accurately   experience and feelings
[143] 4. second stage
[144] 4.1. practical
[145] 4.2 current conflict
[146] 5. mood changes   reactions
[147] 5.1. child   parent   coping
[148] 5.2. points-out

    5.3. There are also _____

        modes in clients.[149]

    5.4. PCL Life Coaches would mention healthy modes that they see in their

        clients, because these modes are _____

        and consistent with _____.[150]

6. The **deepest desires** are those that come from the

_____ and are reflective of what

the person _____, not just an impulsive
reaction, thoughtless response, or to fulfill an unhealthy or evil action.[151]

7. **Actions** are in the _____ of the

PCL Life Coaching change process and follow from _____,
such as the goal of resolving a conflict with a friend through the actions of

_____ to the friend with whom there was conflict,

_____, and _____
for forgiveness.[152]

8. **Virtues** are related to _____, and virtues need to be

_____ in order to carry-out the actions,

such as strengthened _____ in order to
go to the other person and ask for forgiveness.[153]

---

[149] 5.3. healthy
[150] 5.4. positive   character strengths
[151] 6. soul-person   truly wants
[152] 7. third stage   goals   talking   apologizing   asking
[153] 8. actions   strengthened   humility

9. God's or a higher power's ***here and now*** beneficial involvement[VII] in a

client's story means, for example, that a client is _____

_____ of God's gracious and kind presence _____

_____ to the friend and talking to the friend.[154]

10. ***Detachment*** or self-distancing[VIII] refers to how the _____

_____, as the one who makes the choices,

manages the _____ personal
reactions and deceptive messages.[155]

11. The following is a summary list of the *Ten Tasks*, when meeting with

clients, with PCL Life Coaching _____
in bold italics.[156]

The Ten Tasks: How to Lead a Life Coaching Meeting

11.1. Begin the meeting with, "_____ most
important for you to talk about today?"[157]

11.2. Actively listen to the _____ (Basic 2)

using the life coach _____ (Basic 3).[158]

11.3. Understand what clients want and set

_____ (Basic 2).[159]

---

[154] 9. actively aware   while going
[155] 10. immaterial soul-person   material brain's
[156] 11. basic principles
[157] 11.1. What's
[158] 11.2. *story   attitudes*
[159] 11.3. *situational goals*

11.4. Find out what stands in the way of reaching the situational goals,

such as shifting client _____
(see Basic 5).[160]

11.5. Explore, with clients, for their _____
(person-centered godly and positive goals − Basic 2) related to the story.[161]

11.6. Agree on practical _____
(Basic 2) steps to reach goals.[162]

11.7. Identify the related _____
(see Basic 4) that need to be strengthened.[163]

11.8. Provide an explanation about God's _____
involvement in their story or how their higher power can be of benefit.[164]

11.9. Remind clients about using _____
(see Basic 6) — that their persons can manage their brains and bodies.[165]

11.10. As needed, _____ clients about and _____
for them the life coaching concepts and process, especially whenever
they seem confused and unclear.[166]

12. In life coaching meetings, the PCL Life Coach is using these _____

_____ principles or _____
to bring about change in clients.[167]

---

[160] 11.4. *parts* or **modes**
[161] 11.5. **deepest desires**
[162] 11.6. **action**
[163] 11.7. **virtues**
[164] 11.8. **here and now**
[165] 11.9. **detachment**
[166] 11.10. **teach   model**
[167] 12. *Ten Tasks   Life Coaching Basics*

13. While using these principles, PCL Life Coaches are mindful that the

_____ is distinct from the

_____ — that with their encouragement the client's soul-person is able to direct

_____ and _____.[168]

14. PCL Life Coaches are also mindful that their client's self-concept or

_____ is changing — expanding to include their true identity as a _____.[169]

---

[168] 13. soul-person   brain and body   choices   actions
[169] 14. concept of identity   soul-person

IV. Using the Ten Tasks with the Soul-Person Concept of Identity

1. In Thayer's Greek Lexicon definition for the Greek word "*pneuma*" or spirit (the rational soul), there are four soul-person functions listed:

   _____, _____,

   _____, and _____

   (also see Appendix E).[170]

   1.1. Though the brain stores data that can be retrieved and it also autonomously performs certain bodily functions, the

   _____ that comes from the immaterial

   intellect is not in the _____, but

   rather in the _____.[171]

   1.2. The _____ of the soul is consistent

   with the _____ therein, and a

   _____ soul has renewed desires that are consistent with godly or Christlike character qualities or virtues.[172]

   1.3. It is the _____ between alternatives, as a function of the soul-person, that allows the whole

   person to _____ with the

   soul-person's character and _____ contrary reactions of the brain and body.[173]

---

[170] 1. Knowing   Desiring   Deciding   Acting
[171] 1.1. knowing   brain   soul
[172] 1.2. desiring   character   renewed
[173] 1.3. deciding   decide consistently   decide against

1.4. _____ originate either predominately in the soul-person or in the brain and body, and acting that is consistent with the

soul-person's character is an acting out of the _____

and _____ of the soul-person.[174]

2. Throughout the sessions, as the *Ten Tasks* are being utilized, the soul-person

of the client is behind the _____of the story

and the _____ of the life coach's attitudes.[175]

3. Further, the soul-person has been functioning with some quality of

_____ relationship with God or a higher power.[176]

4. The client's soul-person has _____
(virtues) that are to some degree consistent with godliness and with some
measure of strength.[177]

5. Clients can be regularly reminded that the soul-person is able to

_____ from their current reactions
to situational problems and reflexive ways of managing life, in order to make

_____ and take_____ to

improve in effectiveness and _____ in
positive character, thus enhancing resilience in life.[178]

---

[174] 1.4. Actions   authority   animation
[175] 2. telling   experiencing
[176] 3. here and now
[177] 4. character qualities
[178] 5. self-distance   choices   action   grow

6. In _____, the soul-persons of each individual

   are connecting through their use of their own

   _____.[179]

7. Should something interfere with the _____ of

   either or both persons' _____ (e.g., unconsciousness)

   or _____ (e.g., ears), then

   soul-persons would be _____ to fully connect in relationship.[180]

8. One's brain-based _____

   affects what one does in relationships, and an _____
   concept of identity would negatively impact the way the person relates to others.[181]

9. When both people are _____

   adequately in brain and body and with _____

   concepts of their identities, a reasonably good _____
   can be expected between the soul-persons of each.[182]

10. Individuals who have an _____
    of their identity as soul-persons would recognize that character qualities or

    virtues _____ in the soul-person and can be

    used to make _____ and take _____
    with the whole person.[183]

---

[179] 6. relationships   brains and bodies
[180] 7. functioning   brains   bodies   unable
[181] 8. concept of identity   inaccurate
[182] 9. functioning   accurate   connection
[183] 10. accurate concept   originate   choices   action

11. When a PCL Life Coach interacts with a client, there is a

_____of _____

_____, with the virtues of the PCL Life Coach influencing a strengthening of the client's character and positively shifting

the client's _____.[184]

12. The desires of the soul-person are _____ _____ level desires than those in the brain and body, and are reflective of _____ the person really is.[185]

13. The PCL Life Coach can assist clients to _____

themselves better — to _____

with their deeper soul-person desires, and then set _____

and take _____ that fit with these deeper desires.[186]

14. Regenerate individuals would be expected to be able to identify and act out

of their _____ deeper desires that are consistent with Christlikeness.[187]

15. As whole persons, clients can use their soul-persons to challenge what is happening in their brains, and PCL Life Coaches can reinforce clients' concepts of their identities using the following

_____.[188]

---

[184] 11. communicating   character qualities   concept of identity
[185] 12. deeper   who
[186] 13. know   identify   goals   actions
[187] 14. renewed
[188] 15. detachment steps

15.1. **_Relabeling_** — That the _____

and _____ reactions (malfunctions) are

_____ and _____
reactions and not who they really are as soul-persons (though
affecting the whole person).[189]

15.2. **_Reattributing_** — That the dysfunctional and sinful reactions are

_____ (deceptive brain messages)

in the _____ brain and body.[190]

15.3. **_Refocusing_** — By defining these malfunctions (deceptive brain

messages) as _____

from their _____
(though affecting the whole person) and by using their soul-persons

to make healthy, _____
choices instead.[191]

15.4. **_Revaluing_** — That these malfunctions are _____

with their soul-person identity (and _____

of identity), as well as inconsistent with life _____
and flourishing.[192]

---

[189]　15.1. dysfunctional　　sinful　　brain　　body
[190]　15.2. malfunctions　　physical
[191]　15.3. distinct　　soul-persons　　virtue-based
[192]　15.4. inconsistent　　concept　　management

16. The term _____ means that

    clients believe they are able to effectively make _____
    in their lives.[193]

17. Clients can use their _____

    concept of identity to believe more _____
    that they are persons who have authority over their brains and bodies —

    that their soul-persons can more_____ make
    choices and direct their whole persons toward change (also see Appendix G).[194]

18. There is an even greater potential for self-efficacy in regenerate clients, when
    they understand that the functioning of their _____

    soul-persons is distinct from their brain and body functioning — in other
    words, by locating their concept of identity in their soul-persons already

    made _____
    in Christ (i.e., having regenerated natures with more potential for growth in
    virtues consistent with the character of Christ, having been freed from the
    power of sin, and being empowered by the indwelling Holy Spirit).[195]

19. A _____ is a brain-based
    psychological process in which part of the psychological self is cut off, to
    some degree, from other aspects of the psychological self, [IX] but these modes

    are in the _____ and not in the soul-person.[196]

---

[193] 16. self-efficacy   changes
[194] 17. soul-person   strongly   effectively
[195] 18. regenerate   perfect and capable
[196] 19. schema mode   brain

20. Consistent with a _____,
    PCL Life coaches can help clients remember that their soul-persons can

    make _____ by the
    brain-based dysfunctional modes.[197]

---

[197] 20. soul-person concept of identity   choices not hindered

V. The PCL Life Coaching Supervised Practice Experience

1. PCL Life Coaching training also teaches people how to come alongside of

   others in a helpfully _____

   manner, but with using the _____
   (see Appendix K) and not the structured worksheets.[198]

2. To complete the PCL Life Coaching training requires a time of

   _____, with a practice
   client, in order to become skilled in the use of this model of life coaching.
   (This is in addition to the previous 50 of hours PCL Life Mentoring practice
   and 25 hours of PCL Life Mentoring supervision for earning the PCL Life
   Mentoring certificate.)[199]

3. The *Ten Tasks* _____
   is a helpful way to record what happens in these PCL Life Coaching practice
   meetings and is also useful on an ongoing basis when doing PCL Life
   Coaching (see Appendices H and I).[200]

4. The PCL Life Coaching supervised practice includes _____

   _____ with a client and then attending the

   ongoing group and/or individual _____

   _____ (see Appendix M), where trainees talk about the
   life coaching sessions they are having with their clients.[201]

---

[198] 1. intentional and personal   *Ten Tasks*
[199] 2. supervised practice
[200] 3. Meeting Notes Form
[201] 4. practicing life coaching   supervision meetings

5. This post in-class PCL Life Coaching training has the requirement of an

   additional _____ of life coaching practice meetings

   with clients and _____ of group supervision, in order
   to earn the Life Coaching Certificate (see Appendix J).[202]

6. The most significant and essential learning, about how to be an effective

   PCL Life Coach, occurs during the _____ practice.[203]

7. Life Coaching can be practiced _____
   and clients can be charged a fee for service. However, the specific local
   requirements would have to be fulfilled regarding obtaining a business license.[204]

8. Even after training for the PCL Life Coaching certificate has been completed,

   there is a commitment to ongoing _____

   _____ development, through opportunities for continuing

   _____.[205]

---

[202] 5. 50 hours   25 hours
[203] 6. supervised
[204] 7. professionally
[205] 8. learning and skill   education and supervision

APPENDICES

DIAGRAMS

Appendix A: Life Mentoring Process of Change Flow Diagram

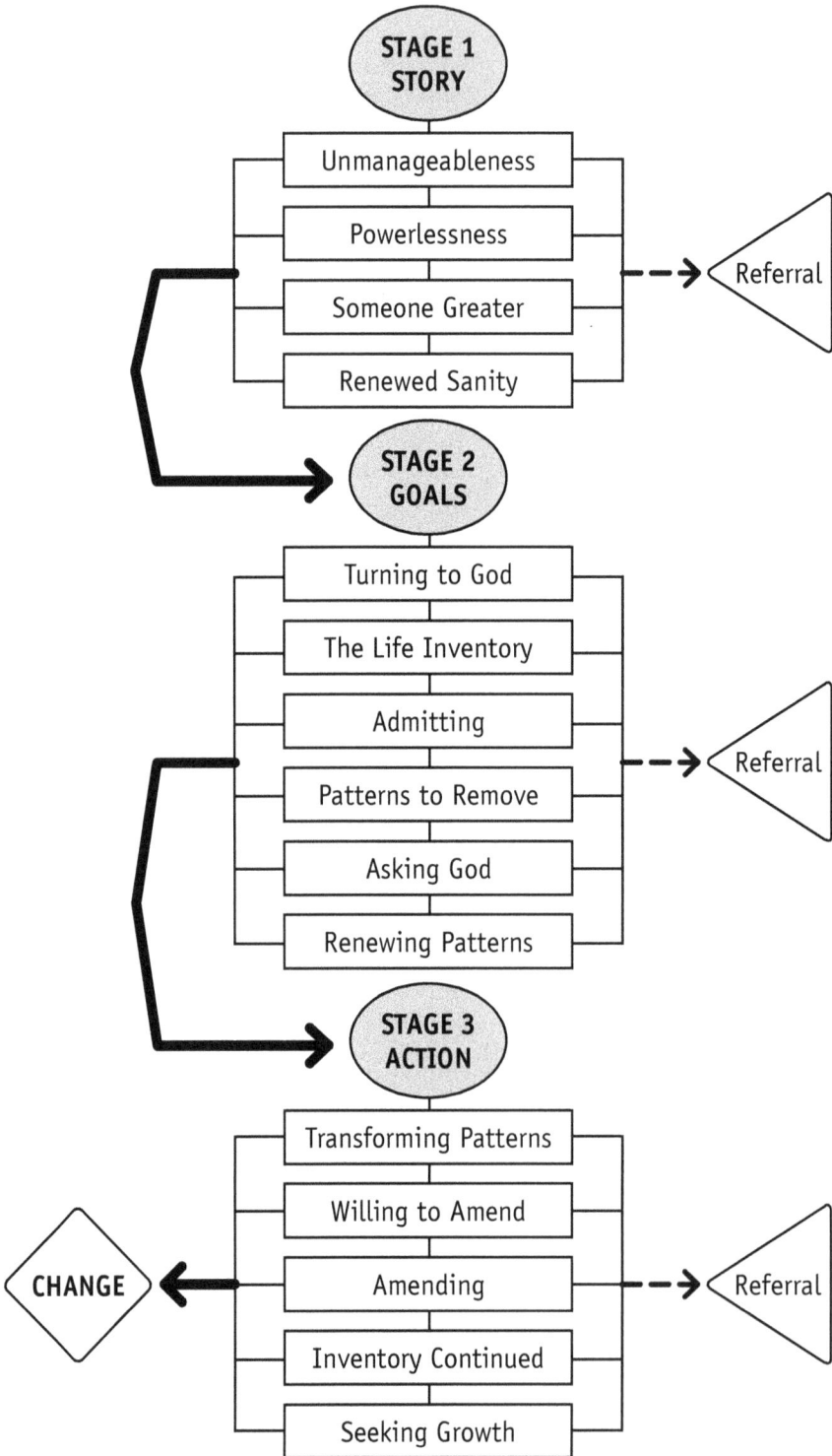

Appendix B: Life Coaching Process of Change Flow Diagram

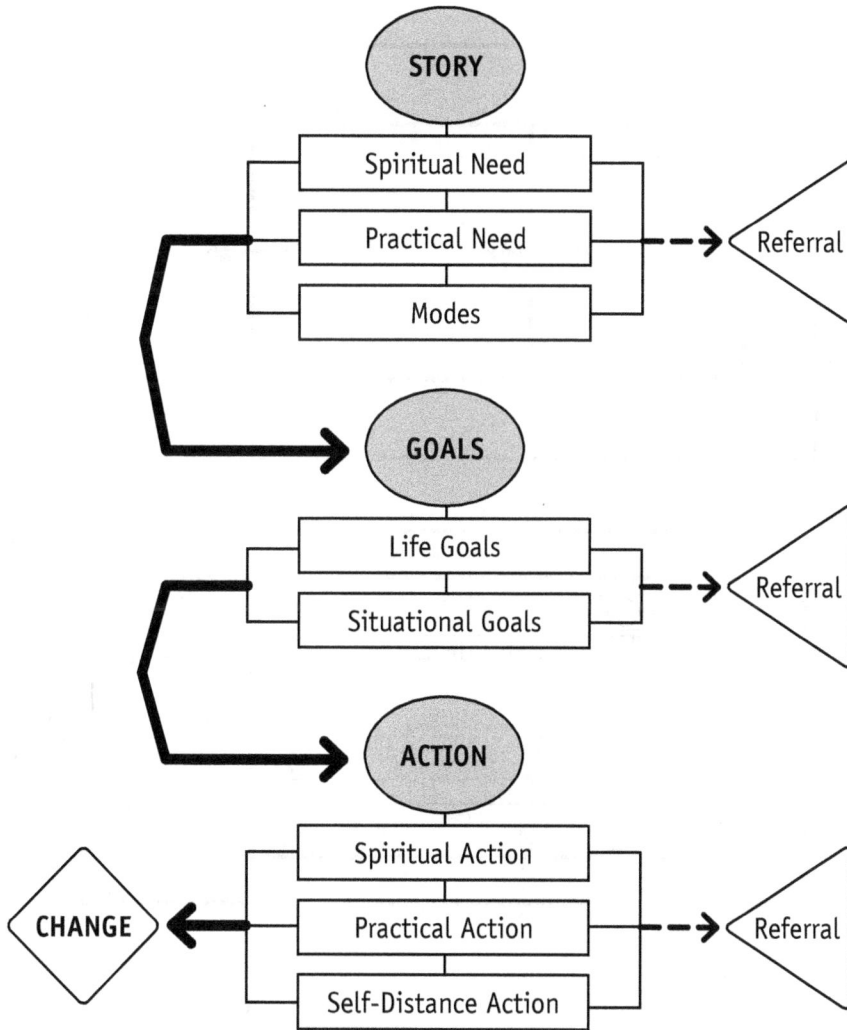

Appendix C: The Whole-Person Illustrated by a Comparison with Solomon's Temple

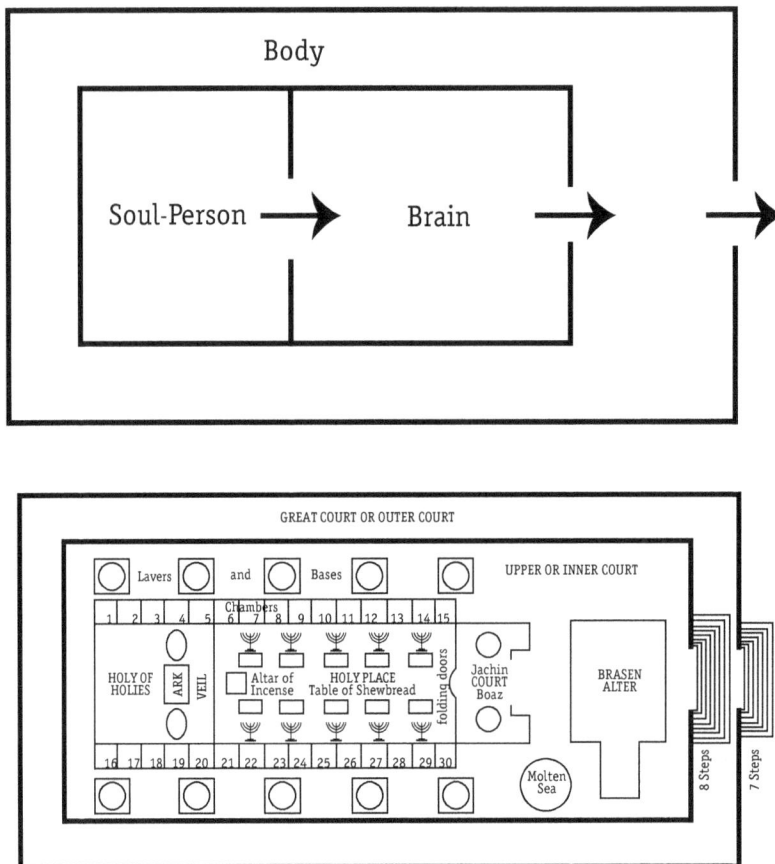

The soul-person is the immaterial person who is the real person, though utilizing the brain and the rest of the body while here on earth. The Holy Spirit empowers *regenerated* soul-persons. The soul-person is expressed though the brain and the rest of the body. This means that the soul-person is having an impact on his/her brain's psychological personality and personality functioning.

FURTHER EXPLANATIONS

Appendix D: Re-Orienting to a Soul-Person Concept of Identity and Owning Who I am

RE-ORIENTING TO A SOUL-PERSON CONCEPT OF IDENTITY AND OWNING WHO I AM

In *Person and Character Level* (PCL) *Life Mentoring and Coaching*[X] intentional change occurs, and this can include a modification to one's personal self-concept or concept of identity. In other words, during the PCL Life Mentoring and Coaching process, clients will likely become increasingly aware of their self-concept and that changes are happening — that their concept of identity is *reorienting*.

The soul-as-the-person view of personal identity is considered a central and significant factor in PCL Life Mentoring and Coaching. This reality has the potential to reshape how clients define their identity — to reorient their identity or self-concept. This reorienting is grounded in their soul being defined as their real person, and other aspects of their concept of identity are then derived from and/or are congruent with this foundational reality. The PCL Life Mentoring and Coaching process is an opportunity and means for clients to clarify their personal concept of identity and consider adopting a soul-person concept of identity. When clients adopt a soul-person concept of identity, there is added potential for them to better manage current situations, grow in the needed character qualities, enhance the use of relational resources, and be more resilient in general to the challenges of life.

This reorienting of clients' concepts of identity will likely be a natural part of the PCL Life Mentoring and Coaching process. It is therefore important to provide PCL Life Coaches with more extensive information, so that they: can have a fuller understanding of identity concepts and of the soul-person concept of identity in particular, can more clearly articulate an explanation of this identity concept to their clients, and are better able to assist their clients in this concept of identity reorienting.

PERSONAL IDENTITY WITHOUT MUCH THOUGHT

We go about our daily lives performing a multitude of actions externally and internally. Every movement, every thought, every moment of every day is performed, for the most part, very routinely and without much thought. But who performs these functions, who initiates them? We are quick to say "I" do them and "I" initiate them. This "I" is who we identify as our person, the concept we have of who we are — our self-concept.

This person that we conceptualize as ourselves is both obvious and illusive. We can simply live our lives and think very little of how we are actually getting ourselves to do things. If curious, we can do an internet search for information on how we do things and there will be references to books and articles and blogs, etc. that claim that this or that region of the brain has been determined through research to control such things as attention and concentration and memory. If there is any mention of something mysterious behind the brain, such as an immaterial soul, such a "ghost in the machine" is mentioned dismissively.

Defining the cause of one's actions as the brain itself leaves the personal identity intact as being purely a result of physical brain activity. Contained in this brain activity is the human personality and more broadly the human self or person. However, there is a nagging difficulty with this seemingly peaceful resolution to the question, "Who am I?". The difficulty is that we have the experience of being more than simply brain processes — we seem to exist as persons — perhaps as a "ghost in the machine". As well, there is no neuroscience explanation as to what or who internally, for instance, "aims the searchlight of attention[XI]". There are areas of the brain that are activated and active when giving attention, but there is still no explanation for what activates the activation of these areas.

So, the identity concept that one has of oneself is missing the explanatory or causative piece for how we do things. This may not be troublesome under normal conditions of daily routines, without challenges. However, there are the not infrequent times in life when there are significant challenges and trials, not only from our outside circumstances and relationships, but also due to internal emotional turmoil and struggle. One's concept of identity is related to how we do things and comes into play in order to adequately and successfully face these external and internal challenges of life. PCL Life Mentoring and Coaching is an intentional relationship, with a process and goals to enhance this coping and resilience, but from a perspective that also utilizes an expanded concept of personal identity.

EXPANDING ONE'S CONCEPT OF PERSONAL IDENTITY

Before launching into a discussion of making a change to one's personal identity concept, it is important to provide a definition for this term *identity concept* or *self-concept*. Osyerman, et. al.[XII] have provided a useful working definition and description of one's self-concept (concept of identity).

Self-concepts are cognitive *structures* that can include content, attitudes, or evaluative judgments and are used to make sense of the world, focus one's attention on goals, and protect one's sense of basic worth..."[XIII]

The concept of one's identity is not the actual self or person, it is rather who one thinks one is and then functions in life accordingly. As can be imagined, this identity concept can both expand and limit what one believes is possible when faced with normal everyday life, as well as with the exceptional challenges of life. Additionally, identity as a self-concept (who one thinks one is) hopefully conforms more rather than less to who the person truly is — to a true, objective identity, as established by outside referents (such as, psychological, philosophical, and theological/biblical views of true personal identity). It is crucial that one's concept of identity be not only accurate, but also thorough and account for all of who the person is. In particular, all the primary dimensions of human existence need to be accounted for. In PCL Life Mentoring and Coaching, human beings are understood to be more than and distinct from their material brain and body processes. The immaterial as well as the material dimensions must both be included in the concept of one's identity.

REORIENTING TO A SOUL-PERSON IDENTITY CONCEPT

The concept of identity reorientation being referred to here is about this all-inclusiveness of dimensions. In particular, in PCL Life Mentoring and Coaching there is an addressing of the reality that there is a spiritual, immaterial dimension to the person's identity. The addition of this spiritual reality, to one's concept of identity, is given definite form because the immaterial soul is explained to be the location of the person, not the physical brain. This immaterial person interacts with, yet has functions beyond and above, the brain and body. A conception of identity shift occurs in PCL Life Mentoring and Coaching clients, as there is an incorporating of the redefinition of their identity. The central identity related concept is that there is a type of "ghost in the machine", and this is more than just a point of view, it is an actual structural reality in human beings. The immaterial soul is considered to be equivalent to the person, though there is also at the same time an acknowledging of psychological processes and functioning occurring within the brain. Defining the soul as being the person and then understanding that it is the soul-person who animates the brain and can effectively influence the brain, contributes positively to a change in clients' concepts of their personal identities.

This change to a soul-person concept of identity is likely to be a quite different experience of oneself and initially feel unnatural for clients. They will more likely have lived thinking that their self or person is contained within the physical structure of their brains and that this limited concept of personal identity is reflective of their real persons. It will be new to clients and perhaps feel foreign to have this reoriented concept of their identity as a soul-person. Furthermore, there can be an increasing realization that their prior concept of their identity was a false construct. It was faulty to previously have their personal identity conceptually located in the brain's composite of memories, beliefs, psychological and physical processes, etc.

It is no small change to begin believing that one has a person distinct from the brain and the rest of the body. However, this concept of identity shift has greater potential for managing one's whole person, than to have had the limited idea that there is no one inside one's whole self who can effectively self-distance from problems and problematic internal psychological processes and make choices and prompt action that moves the brain and body in healthy directions. There are functions of the immaterial soul-person that can be performed with a determinate and authoritative influence (see Appendix E for information on soul-person functions).

FACILITATING THE REORIENTATION TO A SOUL-PERSON CONCEPT OF IDENTITY

This section is about helping clients to make progress in changing their identity concept. Direct and indirect teaching about the soul-person identity concept occurs within the PCL Life Coaching *Ten Tasks*[XIV] process (see Appendix F for connections with specific aspects of the *Ten Tasks*). The direct teaching can happen at various times, but preferably when the conversation involves references to ideas that the client has about himself or herself. This discussion can begin with inviting clients to verbalize their current concept of their identity and then by following-up with a positive dialog. The PCL Life Coach can mention to clients the importance of the concept of identity and how that identity concept can be grounded in the reality of their being an immaterial soul-person. This is the direct, educative approach for assisting in identity concept change. However, it is also important to explore a more indirect, yet powerful and more continuous way to influence self-concept change.

Bergner and Holmes state that the self-concept[XV] (or one's concept of identity) is most usefully defined as a summary of one's position in relation to the rest of the world, including oneself — for example the evaluation of one's own self-worth. This positional-related definition of self-concept is in contrast to the idea that self-concept is just an organized summary of facts about oneself.

Bergner and Holmes recommend helping clients change their self-concepts by relating to them in ways incompatible with client's self-concept, thus communicating a different self-concept to the person. One example of this would be a client who bases her worth on how well she performs and to relate to her in an unconditional positive regard way — communicating a shift in self-concept — that the worth of her person is not based on performance. This is a kind of self-concept status change — a higher status self-concept than had been the client's.

In PCL Life Coaching, clients' self-concepts or identity statuses would be further modified and reinforced by their learning that they are an immaterial soul-person to whom these higher statuses are assigned. It is the soul-person identity concept that is offered to clients as the basis for personal identity. This soul-person identity concept includes the idea that the client has the potential to actualize these statuses. Stated in modified Bergner and Holmes[XVI] terms, the soul-person identity concept would have certain types of statuses. For example, the identity concept statuses would then be that the soul-person:

1. Is acceptable as a person (and for the regenerate, made fully acceptable to God)

2. Makes sense (i.e., is able to make sense of things)

3. Is whose best interests come first in PCL Life Coaching

4. Is who is important and significant to the PCL Life Coach

5. Is who already possesses enabling strengths, knowledge, and other resources for solving problems (this knowledge would be more reliable for the regenerate, in terms of having a new heart, being ready to grow in virtues that are Christlike and therefore congruent with Scriptural truth).

6. Is who will be given the benefit of the doubt (In PCL Life Coaching, this would be understood to mean that, in addition to healthy functioning in the brain, faulty personality functioning is also in the brain, as are the remaining sinful desires of the flesh. So, the soul-person is regarded, under normal conditions, to be the one who has the power to make choices overriding the brain and body — is the one who is given the benefit of the doubt.)

7. Because of this power to make choices, has the agency to not be a victim of internal brain and body functioning or external situations.

As with the Bergner and Holmes' approach to helping clients change their self-concept, the PCL Life Coach assigns these statuses *a priori* (presupposed as true or self-evident). But unlike their view in assigning to a supposed person of the material brain and body, in PCL Life Coaching this assigning of statuses is to the immaterial soul-person who is the client's real and distinct person. One can see the definite advantage, of the PCL Life Coaching understanding of human nature, because the soul-person is not coming from the same brain that holds the self-concept. Thus, the soul-person is able to have a self-distanced vantage point from which to act upon the brain and influence it to reorient to a soul-person concept of identity (see Appendix G for an explanation of advantages related to the soul-person identity concept).

The facilitating of a new identity concept can be communicated through these indirect relational attitudes (e.g., congruence, positive regard, and empathy[XVII]). As mentioned previously, more direct educational means can also be used by the PCL Life Coach. The direct education approach would include: providing information about the soul-person concept of identity and the change process, making personal applications to the client, and in general to continue to reinforce PCL Life Coaching related concepts. The two approaches can and likely will occur together — through the indirect PCL Life Coaching attitudes and by directly educating.

CONCLUDING REMARKS

A soul-person concept of identity does not have to be so foreign, if one considers that a "me" has always been in my awareness and has always been observing. In times of anxiety or depression or internal conflict or any life experience, "I" have always been the observer. It is "I" who has always been observing the whole me, and this same "I" is the "I" who will live in eternity.

One way to consider a reorientation to the soul-person concept of identity is to look at it from this perspective of eternity. Once a person comes into existence, that person is the same person, here on earth, who will eventually pass on into life after death. To more clearly grasp this continuity of existence one can embrace the concept of identity that the soul-person is the real person and the physical brain and body are significant, but not crucial for having consciousness and personhood.

Anything essential for this soul-person identity has to be able to survive death. The brain and body are important for life and are contained in the whole person along with the soul-person, but they are not the location of the soul-person identity. The physical brain and body are the material part of the whole-person identity, are distinct from the immaterial soul, and are the how the soul-person interacts in this earthly life. A soul-person concept of identity resonates with our experience of this condition of being a whole person with two distinct parts.

Of course, for the regenerate person after death there is not eternal disembodiment, but rather the eventual receiving of a new resurrected body. However, receiving this new body does not mean that there will then be some different person. Once again there will be wholeness, but the wholeness of being united with a vessel — a resurrected one that fully resonates effortlessly with the soul-person — the perfect whole-person embodiment for the soul-person.

We do not know extensively what the afterlife experience will be, but from knowing our soul-person concept of identity we can more clearly know the "who" we will be while experiencing it. While in this earthly life, we can become better acquainted with not only our soul-person concept of identity, but by knowing it therefore also become better acquainted with our actual soul-person — the person who will have a continuous existence of identity throughout eternity.

This soul-person concept of identity, along with the personal acknowledgment that the soul-person is the true identity, can be nurtured in clients. They can then better utilize the abilities that their soul-persons have been given and can be open to the continuous development of their soul-persons. On the other hand, to not own who one truly is, is to live inauthentically and contrary to design — as hindered by a faulty self-concept. To own my soul-person identity as the basis for my concept of who I am and to build upon this basis, is an opportunity to live congruently with the original human design, to be unhindered by self-concept, and to be freed to flourish.

Appendix E: Understanding the Functions of the Soul-Person Identity

UNDERSTANDING THE FUNCTIONS OF THE SOUL-PERSON IDENTITY

The soul (or spirit) is the immaterial part of the whole human person and is believed to be the real person or self[XVIII]. This is the concept of identity in PCL Life Coaching. But by stating that the person is the immaterial soul, there is immediately a dilemma of non-concreteness and illusiveness. What functions would be associated with that which is immaterial? The following four functions are listed in Thayer's Greek Lexicon[XIX] definition for the Greek word "*pneuma*" or spirit (the rational soul): Knowing, Desiring, Deciding, and Acting. However, these terms are not specifically described in Thayer's definition. Others[XX] have argued for additional functions, but for the sake of simplicity, our current discussion will focus on the four functions that Thayer's mentions: Knowing, Desiring, Deciding, and Acting.

One could attribute these four functions to the material brain (and body), but their connection with the brain is not necessarily causal, as in the brain originating these functions or being the only cause, or the brain being the ultimate cause of these functions. The brain does know, desire, decide, and act-out through the rest of the body. However, the brain is not the ultimate source of agency or cause for these four functions. The brain is reactive and subject to errors due to faulty learning and execution that limits and distorts, as well as resulting from innate spiritual corruption. There appears to be agency in the brain, but correlation is not causation. There are reactions correlated with and triggered by situations and circumstances, but these functions, when in the brain, are reactions that are not truly causal. The real person, the soul, is always present as the ultimate cause or person with true agency — the immaterial part of the whole person who retains and exercises these functions causally and with self-efficacy.

The immaterial soul-person functions are acted out through the brain and the rest of the material body. However, these functions do not necessarily require a body. (That humans have had no earthly experience of functioning without the material body, does not mean that the immaterial soul, if separated from the material body, cannot continue and perhaps even more freely exercise these functions.) Even the Acting function, which may appear to require a body to perform the acts, can occur as a matter of will — the exertion of the soul and not just as a resulting action of the material brain and body.

In fact, all of these functions are involved in the "determinate" will of the soul-person. The determinate will is the will that has the ultimate authority within the whole person, even though the brain exerts its own "psychological" will or pull in certain reactive directions. So, one could say that the will of the soul-person knows and desires and decides, as well as acts.

Although not perfectly executed in an embodied existence, this soul-based willing authoritatively influences the brain and body. Due to the corruption of both soul and body, in the unregenerate[XXI] person, the soul is incapable of directing the brain and body out of a renewed character — one that has been given new knowledge and desires, and freed decision-making and acting. The person with a regenerated soul is in the position of knowing, desiring, deciding and acting or willing in a manner that is consistent with Christlike character, though still limited by the yet-to-be redeemed brain and body — the condition in this earthly life of already and not-yet.

So what are the explanations for understanding functions of the soul? The following are brief descriptions of the four functions previously mentioned.

KNOWING

Though the brain stores data that can be retrieved and it also autonomously performs certain bodily functions, the knowing that comes from the immaterial intellect[XXII] is not in the brain, but rather in the soul. As well, if one knows God and His Special Revelation, then it is the soul that knows. The brain and body, to the extent they know, is a derivative knowing — a knowing derived from the agency and activation and animation of the soul.

DESIRING

The desiring of the soul is not the same as the desiring of the brain and body, which relates to learning and sensual needs. The desiring of the soul is consistent with the character therein. A renewed soul has renewed desires that are consistent with godly or Christlike character qualities or virtues. Of course, these virtues are in competition and cooperation with, as well as in contradiction to and capable of overriding the brain and other bodily desires.

DECIDING

The ability to self-distance and make choices is possible because there is a distinction between the soul (soul-person) and the brain and body. The immaterial soul-person is able to experience and to observe what is taking place in the material brain and body and to then make choices. It is the deciding between alternatives, as a function of the soul-person, that allows the whole person to act contrary to reactions of the brain and body. The soul-person decides according to the character of the soul-person. A regenerated soul-person would have character, though still developing, that is consistent with godliness. When contrary actions that are not consistent with the character of the soul-person flow out from brain and body reactions, then the question can be asked, "What character qualities or virtues, if present and/or present to a greater degree in the soul-person, would determinatively allow for the carrying-out of the soul-person's choices.

ACTING

Acting originates either predominately in the soul-person or in the brain and body. A thoughtless acting, from the brain and body, would not necessarily be consistent with the soul-person's character. Acting that is consistent with the soul-person's character is an acting out of the agency and animation of the soul-person. The soul-person part of the whole person acts more effectively when there is a use of this structural self-distancing from the brain and body.

The specifying of soul functions is useful when attempting to help clients understand their emerging soul-person concept of personal identity and then in the applying of this concept to their lives. Clients can come to more fully appreciate and utilize their identity — that their souls are the persons who have agency and self-efficacy (determinate will to effectively bring about change) with regard to their brains and bodies.

Appendix F: Further Connections for the Soul-Person Concept of Identity

FUTHER CONNECTIONS FOR THE SOUL-PERSON CONCEPT OF IDENTITY[XXIII]

The immediate context for applying an understanding of the soul-person concept of identity is the Person and Character Level Life Coaching process. It is hoped that clients will be able to generalize their understanding into their daily lives, and PCL Life Coaches can assist in this generalization. However, it may not be readily apparent how the soul-person concept of identity connects with the various aspects of PCL Life Coaching. Time will be spent, in this section, explaining some of these connections.

An underlying reality, for the life coach to continually keep in mind, is the perspective of the client being both an ***immaterial person*** and a ***material brain and body***, yet also a whole person. The life coach understands that his immaterial soul-person and the client's immaterial soul-person are the conscious beings who are interacting in the life coaching meetings. Though each individual's material brain and body are involved, immaterial soul-persons are animating them.

Whatever is happening in the meetings, in either the life coach or the client, is originating within these immaterial soul-persons. This is significant especially for the client, because it means that what occurs in the brain and body of the client is at least potentially subject to the authority of the client's soul-person. The brain and body of the client may exert a substantial force, but in normal functioning people, it is the person who has the actual agency (the capacity to act independently). The soul-person of the client is who the life coach is addressing and encouraging to be engaged in the process of life coaching.

CONNECTION WITH THE *TEN TASKS*

Throughout the sessions, as the *Ten Tasks*[XXIV] are being utilized, there is involvement potential for the client's soul-person. For example, the soul-person of the client is behind the telling of the story and the experiencing of the life coach's attitudes. Further, the soul-person has been functioning with some quality of here and now relationship with God or a higher power, and the client's soul-person has character qualities (virtues) that are to some degree consistent with godliness and with some measure of strength. Clients can be regularly reminded of this by the life coach, along with the encouragement to remember that the soul-person is able to self-distance from the client's current reactions to situational problems and reflexive ways of managing life, in order to make choices and take action to improve in effectiveness and grow in positive character, thus enhancing resilience in life.

CONNECTION WITH RELATIONSHIPS

When interacting with another, the soul-persons of each individual are connecting through their use of their own brains and bodies. Should something interfere with the functioning of either or both persons' brains (e.g., unconsciousness) or bodies (e.g., ears), then soul-persons would be unable to fully connect in relationship. As well, an inaccurate concept of identity would negatively impact the way the person relates to others. Since one's concept of identity affects what one does in relationships, the soul-person concept of identity (SPCI) is significantly implicated and connected with relationships. When both people are functioning adequately in brain and body and with accurate concepts of their identities, a reasonably good connection can be expected between the soul-persons of each. However, adequate functioning is not perfect functioning, so there is always the potential for misunderstandings, misinterpretations, and miscommunication between the two people.

What is true of the way human relationships are done is likely also characteristic of the person's relationship with God or a higher power. Improvements in being able to experience the relationship with the life coach will facilitate improvements in client's ability to make healthier connects with God or a higher power.

CONNECTION WITH CHARACTER

Individuals who have a clearer concept of their identity as soul-persons would recognize that character qualities or virtues originate in the soul-person and can be used to make choices and take action with the whole person. Character in the regenerate soul-person is enhanced because the person has been given a renewed nature that is consistent with Christlikeness, though in need of being strengthened. As well, the regenerate soul-person has been freed from the power of sin, and the Holy Spirit is present and empowering.

Brain and body, when functioning within normal limits, would be assumed to allow for the communicating of virtues, if not verbally then at least in behavior within the relationship with the life coach. The soul-person of one individual is communicating character qualities to the other. When it is a PCL Life Coach communicating with a client, then the virtues of the Life Coach would be influencing the client toward growth in character.

Improvements to being able to relate to the character of the life coach and then to the character of God, are enhanced as the client's character qualities increase. The more consistent the client's character is with godliness (Christlike), the more the client will naturally resonate with the character of God and be able to experience God's active here and now involvement in a way that is consistent with God's character.

CONNECTION WITH SITUATIONAL GOALS AND ACTIONS

When the SPCI is operating effectively, the person will recognize the difference between a deeper desire from within the soul-person and a desire from within the physical brain and body. The desire of the regenerate soul-person will be in the direction of godliness, though this same person's brain and body-based desires may or may not yet be godly. However, the desires of the soul-person are deeper level desires than those in the brain and body. The PCL Life Coach can explore with the client to further clarify these deeper desires, of the soul-person, and then with the client set goals and actions to fit with these deeper desires. These regenerate individuals would be expected to be able to identify and act out of their renewed deeper desires that are consistent with Christlikeness. Unregenerate individuals, not having their soul-person desires renewed, not being freed from the power of sin, and not having the Holy Spirit's empowerment could not be expected to be as consistent. They may have godly deeper desires and be able to act out of them, because of common grace, but it would not be a given, because they do not have a soul-person who has been regenerated.

CONNECTION WITH BRAIN MANAGEMENT

The type of brain management being referred to is that which makes a clear distinction between what is happening in the brain and the rest of the body and that which is the real soul-person. Life Coaches can encourage their clients to address these personal issues and reactions. As whole persons, clients can use their soul-persons to challenge what is happening in their brains. Life Coaches can teach and apply and continue to remind clients of their soul-person identities and the use of the following detachment steps.[xxv] The detachment steps[xxvi] include:

1. **Relabeling** — That the dysfunctional and sinful reactions (malfunctions) are brain and body reactions and not who they are as soul-persons (though affecting the whole person).

2. **Reattributing** — That the dysfunctional and sinful reactions are malfunctions (deceptive brain messages) in the physical brain and body.

3. **Refocusing** — By defining these malfunctions (deceptive brain messages) as distinct from their soul-persons (though affecting the whole person) and by using their soul-persons to make healthy, virtue-based choices instead.

4. **Revaluing** — That these malfunctions are inconsistent with their soul-person identity and inconsistent with life management and flourishing.

CONNECTION WITH SELF-EFFICACY

The term self-efficacy, as used here, means that clients believe they are able to effectively make changes in their lives. The obvious connection between this and the soul-person identity concept is that clients use this concept to believe more strongly that they are persons who are distinct from their brain and body functioning. They (in their soul-persons) can therefore believe that they have more authority over their brains and bodies. Because their soul-persons are in their whole persons, but are not located in their brains, their soul-persons can more effectively make choices and direct their whole persons toward change.

An even greater potential for self-efficacy, within whole persons, is possible when it is the functioning of a regenerate soul-person that is in distinction with the brain and body's functioning. In other words, regenerate clients can come to understand and utilize this clearer distinction in functioning by locating their concept of identity in their soul-persons already made perfect in Christ (regenerated natures with more potential for growth in virtues consistent with the character of Christ, having been freed from the power of sin, and being empowered by the indwelling Holy Spirit). The regenerate soul-person, with its determinate will toward efficacy, becomes the basis for the person's concept of identity, rather than the psychological and physical functioning within the brain and body.

CONNECTION WITH MODES — THE SHIFTING PSYCHOLOGICAL PARTS[XXVII]

A schema mode is a brain-based psychological process in which part of the psychological self is cut off, to some degree, from other aspects of the psychological self. There are dysfunctional modes[XXVIII] (child, parent, and coping) and there are healthy modes as well. Though modes can be quite powerful and disturbing, they are merely psychological. This is not to minimize the influence of modes, especially as an uncontrolled influence, but to put modes into proper perspective. Modes are not the soul-person. Modes are in the brain's psychological functioning. Life Coaches can help all clients remember that their soul-persons can make choices (using their soul-person determinate wills). In other words, their soul-persons are capable of influencing these brain-based psychological modes and have the potential to make choices not hindered by the dysfunctional modes. It is additionally important to keep in mind that when clients are regenerate, the character of their soul-persons has been renewed and is growing in godly virtues. They have also been freed from the power of sin, and the Holy Spirit is available in them to strengthen their soul-persons to be better able to influence whole-person functioning. A soul-person concept of identity allows individuals to more fully recognize that effective choices can be made, in spite of the brain's dysfunction modes and/or in cooperation with the brain's healthy modes.

Appendix G: Advantages of the Soul-Person Identity Concept

ADVANTAGES OF THE SOUL-PERSON IDENTITY CONCEPT[xxix]

PROVIDING A MORE SOLID FOUNDATION FOR HOPE

When human nature is poorly understood as a muddled mixture of internal processes, it is difficult for people to get a clear sense of their soul-person identity apart from contaminated inner processes. When a person is in Christ, this confusion inhibits both a sense of being solidly new in Christ and being perfectly prepared to make progress in life. The effects of regeneration, justification, and sanctification should be understood as providing a solid new person who is enabled by the Holy Spirit to influence the brain and body, thus directing the whole person to being more consistently Christ-like. Seeing oneself in this manner (i.e., having a soul-person concept of identity) both grounds and increases hope — a hope that one can experience change and in fact will be changed — hope having a sense of self-efficacy.

ALLOWING FOR CHOICE

The perhaps unintentional consequence of an unclear view of the soul-person versus the brain and body, is to put limitations on the perceived ability to choose. When both unregenerate as well as regenerate persons are able to affirm having an immaterial person, then they are further enabled to have a concept of identity that has with it the ability to make choices over internal processes and external behaviors of the material part of their whole persons. Regenerate persons, having a clear understanding that their soul-persons are distinct from their brain and body functioning, are enabled potentially to an even greater extent to enact the choices that can be made, because of also being freed from the power of sin and empowered by the Holy Spirit.

MORE HONESTY THAT COMES FROM ASSURANCE AND DETACHMENT

Hiding imperfect aspects of oneself and behavior from others is a self-protective attempt to keep from being unacceptable to another. When one's self-concept includes the idea of worth as based primarily in performance, this is also a negative self-confirmation — self-confirming unacceptableness. However, if clients know intellectually and personally that they are unconditionally accepted (unconditionally positively regarded), then there is freedom from the fear of being unacceptable. A basis for the courage to be honest can be additionally derived and strengthened from the assurance of being a fully redeemed and accepted person in Christ, even while still having imperfections in the performance of the brain and body. This inclusion in one's concept of identity as being a redeemed child of God can then bring with it an assurance of acceptableness and a willingness to be more honest in the self-assessment of ongoing sinfulness and weakness. Because one can more honestly reveal imperfections when one is secure about being accepted by the other, communication can be more open. With greater personal awareness, admission of imperfections and confession of the shortcomings, while assured of acceptance, there can be a fuller cooperation with others toward personal and spiritual growth. This is the case in one's relationship with God as well, where the varied internal sanctification issues can be more extensively and fully addressed.

CLEARER PERSPECTIVE ON THE INTERNAL STRUGGLE

If the person can internally step his/her soul-person back from an internal psychological conflict and view the place where the battle is raging as in the brain, then there is a valuable perspective from which to move forward. This self-distancing is made even more effective for regenerate individuals, because there is a soul-person "me" who will be strengthened by the Holy Spirit, and the combined "we" of the soul-person and the Holy Spirit will together address the brain-based internal psychological conflict. Regenerate soul-persons can address the struggle in their brains with a positive, self-distanced concept of their identity. Rather than approaching the internal conflict from a negative self-concept that says, "I am the badness I seek to defeat", the regenerate soul-person approaches the struggle by acknowledging that, "I am the new person enabled to defeat the non-person remaining imperfections".

LOCATION AND REALITY OF PSYCHOLOGICAL PROCESSES AND PROBLEMS

In the soul-person concept of identity put forth here, humans are viewed as having a material part (the brain and the rest of the body) and an immaterial part (the soul or spirit) to their whole person, and the soul or spirit is the person. For the regenerate person, remaining sinfulness is understood to reside in the material part of the whole-person, i.e., in the brain and body. This could be misunderstood, with regard to the regenerate soul-person, to be saying that since sin has been eradicated, in the person (soul/spirit) by regeneration, then all that remains to be done can be accomplished through psychotherapy — the solution needed for repairing the problems remaining in the brain and body. This faulty conclusion may come from a difficulty understanding that there is still a sin problem — validating that even though the soul-person is already redeemed by regeneration, there is still a need for forgiveness and growth toward Christ-likeness. In this sense, there is also a concept of the whole person that both acknowledges the soul-person concept of identity, while also acknowledging a brain and body concept of continued sinfulness and psychological dysfunction (psychopathology).

This concept of the whole person locates the psychological problems in the material brain and body — an important perspective for self-efficacy both spiritually and psychologically. As indicated previously, there is more empowerment of this self-efficacy when it is understood that one's soul-person is distinct from one's brain and body, and the soul-person can make choices to affect change in the brain and body. Additional recognition of this empowerment for the soul-person self-efficacy can occur when regenerated individuals understand that not only is their soul-person distinct from their brain and body, but that their soul-person has been made perfect in Christ, is freed from the power of sin, and has the strengthening of the Holy Spirit.

FORMS

Appendix H: Meeting Notes Form

Meeting Notes Form
Person and Character Level (PCL) Life Coaching
TEN TASKS

CLIENT NAME:	DATE:
IMPORTANT TOPICS DISCUSSED:	
CLIENT STORY CONTENT:	LIFE COACH ATTITUDES:
DEEPEST DESIRES IDENTIFIED:	
SITUATIONAL GOALS	
SITUATIONAL GOALS SET:	SITUATIONAL ACTIONS TO TAKE:
LIFE GOALS	
VIRTUES PRESENT AND NEEDED:	
HERE AND NOW RELATING WITH GOD:	
MODES AND BARRIERS TO CHANGE:	
ISSUES FOR DETACHMENT:	
OTHER CONTENT TAUGHT AND MODELED:	
SOUL-PERSON CONCEPT OF IDENTITY	
PRIOR CONCEPT OF IDENTITY:	
REORIENTED CONCEPT OF IDENTITY:	

Appendix I: Meeting Notes Form Completed Example

Meeting Notes Form Completed Example
Person and Character Level (PCL) Life Coaching
TEN TASKS

CLIENT NAME: Mary Smith	DATE: 6.June.2017
IMPORTANT TOPICS DISCUSSED: Conflict with emotionally draining friend	
CLIENT STORY CONTENT: Mary's friend seems to always be in need and wanting her time. Mary has never told her friend directly, but recently snapped at her friend in a conversation — now there's tension.	LIFE COACH ATTITUDES: Positive regard, empathy, and genuineness expressed. Hopeful of her having courage, patience and kindness.
DEEPEST DESIRES IDENTIFIED: Though frustrated with her friend and wanting to keep distance from and not interact with / avoid her friend, at a deeper level, Mary loves her friend and wants to repair the relationship.	
SITUATIONAL GOALS	
SITUATIONAL GOALS SET: 1. Repair the relationship. 2. To not feel taken-advantage-of / drained.	SITUATIONAL ACTIONS TO TAKE: 1. Talk openly with her friend about the recent "snapping" and ask friend for forgiveness. 2. Discuss boundaries with friend (confronting kindly).

LIFE GOALS

VIRTUES PRESENT AND NEEDED:

Mary has had difficulty being assertive with her friend, for fear that her friend won't understand/react badly. She will have to have the <u>courage</u> to speak openly. Mary's become frustrated with her friend's unawareness, so Mary will need have increased <u>patience</u> and <u>kindness</u>. Since there are no guarantees that her friend will understand and respond well, Mary will need to be at <u>peace</u> with the potential outcomes.

HERE AND NOW RELATING WITH GOD:

Mary typically does not think about God being with her in conversations with others and consequently doesn't remember that the outcome also includes God's involvement. She is willing to practice remembering God's positive presence before, during, and after the confrontation with her friend.

MODES AND BARRIERS TO CHANGE:

Mary tends to retreat into a frightened little girl mode when she has to confront others and instead of setting limits, lets herself be used.

ISSUES FOR DETACHMENT:

Mary gets caught-up in the fearful thoughts on the one hand and the frustrated, angry reactions on the other, while usually keeping this all inside and letting it build up because of believing that she would be "bad" if she didn't let people have what they wanted. She needs to see this process as a learned way of reacting in her brain and determinedly choose to take positive action. She needs, further, to remind herself that she is capable of making these choices/ that she is an adult who can take care of herself and will be able to with God's help (self-efficacy).

OTHER CONTENT TAUGHT AND MODELED:

As Mary experiences the patience and kindness of the PCL Life Coach, while discussing the issues directly with her, she will be seeing virtues in action. Mary may need more information about who her real person is and that her reactions in her brain are not really her person. She may additionally need to learn from examples, such as Jesus setting limits with others and his allowing himself to go to the cross was a choice — not done out of passively letting others have control.

SOUL-PERSON CONCEPT OF IDENTITY
PRIOR CONCEPT OF IDENTITY: Seeing herself as a person who cannot stand up for herself and who is overcome by her fear of others and believes that her attempts to resolve conflict will go badly.
REORIENTED CONCEPT OF IDENTITY: Seeing herself more as a person who desires peace and has the courage to make choices, even when fearful, and to take action to confront others, knowing that God is with her.

Appendix J: Life Mentoring and Life Coaching Supervised Practice Recording Form

**Life Mentoring and Life Coaching
Supervised Practice Recording Form**

Month/ Year	Hours of Individual Practice	Hours of Group Practice	Hours of Individual Supervision	Hours of Group Supervision	Totals

NAME: DATE:

Type of Hours
Collected: Life Mentoring   Life Coaching

TOOLS

Appendix K: Life Coaching Key Points and *Ten Tasks* Protocol

Life Coaching Key Points and *Ten Tasks* Protocol

Three Primary Life Goals:

1. To strengthen the here and now (real-time) relationship the other person has with God.

2. Encourage growth in character (virtue development).

3. Improved personal coping and resilience.

Three Stages of Change:

1. Telling Their Story.

2. Setting Situational Goals.

3. Taking Action.

The Ten Tasks:

1. Begin the meeting with, "What's most important for you to talk about today?"

2. Actively listen to the **story** using the life coach **attitudes**.

3. Understand what clients want and set **situational goals**.

4. Find out what stands in the way of reaching the situational goals, such as shifting client **parts or modes**.

5. Explore, with clients, for their **deepest desires** (person-centered godly and positive goals) related to the story.

6. Agree on practical **action** steps to reach goals.

7. Identify the related **virtues** that need to be strengthened.

8. Provide an explanation about God's *here and now* involvement in their story or how their higher power can be of benefit.

9. Remind clients about using *detachment* — that their persons can manage their brains and bodies.

10. As needed, *teach* clients about and *model* for them the life coaching concepts and process, especially whenever they seem confused and unclear.

Appendix L: Format for Life Mentoring Practice Meetings

Format for Life Mentoring Practice Meetings

Pre-Meeting Format

- Connect with client briefly to explain the format of meetings:

  1. Opening Check-in.

  2. Summary Points covered and discussion.

  3. Processing Questions discussed.

  4. Characteristic God Responses discussed and applied.

  5. Ending prayer and assignments given.

- Explain that there will be 15 weekly meetings, each 1.5 hours long and covering one *Life in Process* worksheet in each meeting.

- Assign the first *Life in Process* worksheet (either from the regular worksheets or the revised worksheets for the Not-Consciously-Christian).

- Explain that it is best if the client reads over the worksheet and completes the *Processing Questions* prior to each meeting.

- Explain that supervision will be separate from, but concurrent with the life mentoring meetings and confidential.

- Schedule the next meeting time and location.[206]

---

[206] If you choose to use the *Life in Process* book, you would: explain that the first 15 chapters of *Life in Process* will be covered and then assign the first *Life in Process* reading along with the first worksheet (stating that it is best if the client reads the book chapter and/or reads over the worksheet and completes the worksheet *Processing Questions* prior to each meeting).

Meeting Format[207]

1. Opening check-in: Life Mentor asks for client's brief comments on how the material was for her/him.

2. Summary Points covered and discussion: Life Mentor briefly covers the Summary Points on the Worksheet and asks for reactions (listening for the client's story).

3. Processing Questions discussed: Life Mentor presents the questions and listens to the client's responses and makes brief summary comments (further listening for the story, considering practical and virtue goals, and possible actions).

4. Characteristic God Responses discussed and applied: Life Mentor presents the God responses for client to consider and assists client application.

5. Ending prayer (with Consciously-Christian clients), next worksheet assignment given, and next session scheduled.

---

[207] Having a format helps the life mentor to consistently facilitate the client talking. Once the client is used to the format, then the mentor won't need to provide as much direction. Also, notes can be made during or after the meeting, as reminders for the next meeting and for supervision purposes.

Appendix M: Guidelines for Supervision and Case Presentations

Guidelines for Supervision and Case Presentations

The following is information on and a suggested format for making the supervision meetings more defined, focused, and productive.

I. Supervision Defined

Supervision for PCL Life Mentoring and Coaching practice is similar to that of professional clinical practice training.[208] Supervision is a time for Life Mentors or Coaches to openly talk about their work with a client and receive feedback, training, and support that will add to the competence and character of the Life Mentor or Coach.

II. Focusing on Content and Process in Supervision

A. Client Content: information that the client reports happening in current everyday life situations and talks about in the meetings — the client's story in an informational sense.

B. Client Process: the thoughts, feelings, beliefs, and inner reactions the client describes from everyday life and what is seen during the practice time — the client's story in a processes sense.

C. Life Mentor or Coach Process: the thoughts, feelings, beliefs, and inner reactions of the Life Mentor or Coach during the practice time and on reflection outside the meetings — the Life Mentor or Coach's reactions to the client, as a process within.

D. Life Mentor or Coach Content: information and comments made to the client by the Life Mentor or Coach, during the practice meetings.

III. Supervision Meeting Format

---

[208] Professional clinical training supervision is: "a process whereby a person in a supervisory role facilitates the professional growth of one or more designated supervisees to help them attain knowledge, improve their skills, and strengthen their professional attitudes and values as they provide clinical services to their clients." Cohen, *Clinical Supervision: What to Do and How to Do It*, 3.

A. First time a client is presented: client's pseudo name, some demographics, why the client came to see you, what's the initial issue/s to talk about, a brief summary of the client's current life (where living, working, kind of relationships), basic background information.

B. For follow-up presentations of the client: update on progress in the Life Mentoring or Coaching (e.g., what chapter is being worked on or response to the *Ten Tasks*, the client's reactions, mentor or coach's reactions to the client, or overall way the meetings are going).

C. In the group supervision each person will typically have about 15-30 minutes to present. (Please select the most relevant and significant information.)

D. The supervisor will listen, ask questions for clarification, answer questions, and will be giving input.

E. Other group supervision members can feel free to make comments as well. This is an interactive time in which people learn from both the supervisor and each other.

Appendix N: Biblical Character Virtues and Virtues in Action (VIA) Classification of Character Strengths

Biblical Character Virtues
(With works of the flesh found in Galatians)

I CORINTHIANS 13:4-13
Faith

Hope

Love: patient, kind, not envying or boasting, not arrogant or rude, does not insist on its own way, is not irritable or resentful, does not rejoice at wrongdoing, but rejoices with truth, bears all things, believes all things, hopes all things, endures all things, never ends.

COLOSSIANS 3:12-16
Compassion

Kindness

Humility

Meekness

Patience

Bearing others

Forgiving

Thankful

GALATIANS 5:22-23
(Love)[209]

Joy

Peace

(Patience)

(Kindness)

Goodness

Faithfullness

Gentleness

Self-control

sexual immorality	impurity
sensuality	idolatry
sorcery	enmity
strife	jealousy
fits of anger	rivalries
dissensions	divisions
envy	drunkenness
orgies	

The Works of the Flesh – Gal. 5:19-21
Not becoming conceited, provoking one another, envying one another. Gal. 5:26

---

[209] Parentheses indicate that the virtue has already been listed in a prior passage, so is being repeated.

ROMANS 5:3-4
Endurance
(Hope)

II PETER 1:5-9
(Faith)
Excellence
Knowledge
(Self-control)
Steadfastness

The VIA Classification of Character Strengths[210]

1. **Wisdom and Knowledge** — Cognitive strengths that entail the acquisition and use of knowledge

   - *Creativity* [originality, ingenuity]: thinking of novel and productive ways to conceptualize and do things; includes artistic achievement but is not limited to it

   - *Curiosity* [interest, novelty-seeking, openness to experience]: taking an interest in ongoing experience for its own sake; finding subjects and topics fascinating; exploring and discovering

   - *Judgment* [critical thinking]: thinking things through and examining them from all sides; not jumping to conclusions; being able to change one's mind in light of evidence; weighing all evidence fairly

   - *Love of Learning*: mastering new skills, topics, and bodies of knowledge, whether on one's own or formally; obviously related to the strength of curiosity but goes beyond it to describe the tendency to add systematically to what one knows

   - *Perspective* [wisdom]: being able to provide wise counsel to others; having ways of looking at the world that make sense to oneself and to other people.

---

[210] VIA Institute on Character. *The VIA Classification of Character Strengths.*

2. **Courage** — Emotional strengths that involve the exercise of will to accomplish goals in the face of opposition, external or internal

- *Bravery* [valor]: not shrinking from threat, challenge, difficulty, or pain; speaking up for what is right even if there is opposition; acting on convictions even if unpopular; includes physical bravery but is not limited to it

- *Perseverance* [persistence, industriousness]: finishing what one starts; persisting in a course of action in spite of obstacles; "getting it out the door"; taking pleasure in completing tasks

- *Honesty* [authenticity, integrity]: speaking the truth but more broadly presenting oneself in a genuine way and acting in a sincere way; being without pretense; taking responsibility for one's feelings and actions

- *Zest* [vitality, enthusiasm, vigor, energy]: approaching life with excitement and energy; not doing things halfway or halfheartedly; living life as an adventure; feeling alive and activated.

3. **Humanity** — Interpersonal strengths that involve tending and befriending others

- *Love*: valuing close relations with others, in particular those in which sharing and caring are reciprocated; being close to people

- *Kindness* [generosity, nurturance, care, compassion, altruistic love, "niceness"]: doing favors and good deeds for others; helping them; taking care of them

- *Social Intelligence* [emotional intelligence, personal intelligence]: being aware of the motives and feelings of other people and oneself; knowing what to do to fit into different social situations; knowing what makes other people tick.

4. **Justice** — Civic strengths that underlie healthy community life

- *Teamwork* [citizenship, social responsibility, loyalty]: working well as a member of a group or team; being loyal to the group; doing one's share

- *Fairness*: treating all people the same according to notions of fairness and justice; not letting personal feelings bias decisions about others; giving everyone a fair chance

- *Leadership*: encouraging a group of which one is a member to get things done and at the time maintain time good relations within the group; organizing group activities and seeing that they happen.

5. **Temperance** — Strengths that protect against excess

- *Forgiveness*: forgiving those who have done wrong; accepting the shortcomings of others; giving people a second chance; not being vengeful

- *Humility*: letting one's accomplishments speak for themselves; not regarding oneself as more special than one is

- *Prudence*: being careful about one's choices; not taking undue risks; not saying or doing things that might later be regretted

- *Self-Regulation* [self-control]: regulating what one feels and does; being disciplined; controlling one's appetites and emotions.

6. **Transcendence** — Strengths that forge connections to the larger universe and provide meaning

- *Appreciation of Beauty and Excellence* [awe, wonder, elevation]: noticing and appreciating beauty, excellence, and/or skilled performance in various domains of life, from nature to art to mathematics to science to everyday experience

- *Gratitude*: being aware of and thankful for the good things that happen; taking time to express thanks

- **Hope** [optimism, future-mindedness, future orientation]: expecting the best in the future and working to achieve it; believing that a good future is something that can be brought about

- *Humor* [playfulness]: liking to laugh and tease; bringing smiles to other people; seeing the light side; making (not necessarily telling) jokes

- *Spirituality* [faith, purpose]: having coherent beliefs about the higher purpose and meaning of the universe; knowing where one fits within the larger scheme; having beliefs about the meaning of life that shape conduct and provide comfort.[xxx]

WORKSHEETS

Appendix O: Life in Process Worksheets

Life in Process

UNMANAGEABLENESS
Worksheet 1

Summary Points

1. Unmanageable is defined as a life that is out of control in some certain personal areas of one's life or more generally in all areas.

2. Unmanageableness can be identified by noticing areas of over-attention.

3. Unmanageableness is being demonstrated if something or someone negatively consumes large quantities of time and energy and limits the person.

4. Unmanageableness takes away from the quality of relationship with God.

5. Unmanageableness hinders trust in God.

6. When life is out of control, it is difficult to experience God's loving care.

Processing Questions

1. At what point does your life seem out of control?

2. What emotions does being out of control produce in you?

3. What do you tend to do when you get to this point?

4. What advantages are there to finally "hitting bottom" and realizing life is out of control?

5. How do you think God looks at you when your life is out of control?

6. How does this affect whether you come to Him or not?

7. In what dark rooms of your life is God beginning to turn on a light?

Characteristic God Responses

1. God sees and understands the unmanageableness.

2. God's love is extended even while life seems out of control.

3. The unmanageableness blocks the experience of God's loving care.

4. God is actively involved, even when not experienced by the person, and He is working toward exposing the reasons for the unmanageableness.

Life in Process

POWERLESSNESS
Worksheet 2

Summary Points

1. When we find that our lives are unmanageable in some areas, we're faced with what to do about it.

2. The result is that we may try many ways to cope.

3. Here are some typical ways people try to cope, but they are not true solutions.

Drug/alcohol addiction	Dependency on others
Overeating	Focusing on helping others
Working too hard	Controlling others
Numbing out	

4. We are powerless to control everything that happens to us — to change every life circumstance.

5. We are to some extent forced to depend on other people and other things.

6. Dependence must be approached carefully. No other person is safe enough and powerful enough to handle our complete dependence.

7. No thing (e.g., money, possessions, drugs, etc.) can rightfully be an object of our ultimate trust.

8. Negative feelings about being dependent are common, especially for those who have experienced being hurt while depending on others.

9. Being dependent itself is not harmful when we depend appropriately upon someone safe.

10. It is safe to depend on God, without hesitation, because He is both all-good

and all-powerful.

11. Being powerless is a condition of being human, because there are areas of our lives where we cannot manage completely on our own — not having the needed resources or power.

12. God, who created us, knows this need to depend and desires to be the one on whom we trust completely.

13. While we move toward depending on Him more completely, there are other people and things that we are tempted to misuse against the powerlessness.

14. The situation is one of being powerless (i.e., not all-powerful) and in need of finding appropriate ways to be dependent.

Processing Questions

1. Where have you recognized powerlessness in your own life?

2. What emotional responses do you encounter when you personally confront your own powerlessness?

3. How might you be like the younger son, in the parable of the lost son (Luke 15:11), who chose to be on his own and to live his own way?

4. What things have you used to maintain the feeling of power and deny powerlessness?

5. What healthy ways have you learned to express your dependency in a time of need

6. In which areas do you have difficulty depending on God and His power?

Characteristic God Responses

1. God is aware of the alternatives used to cope.

2. He is gracious and patient as the person struggles with trying to cope.

3. He knows that the person needs to depend on him primarily.

4. God is active in the process of the person coming out of denial about powerlessness.

Life in Process

BELIEF IN SOMEONE GREATER THAN MYSELF
Worksheet 3

Summary Points

1. This belief in someone greater than ourselves has various aspects.

2. God is more powerful in the sense of physical strength.

3. The greater than ourselves also applies to His character: all-powerful and all-good.

4. Doubts about God's power and goodness (His being a loving God) undermine trust in Him.

5. When doubt is present, it is difficult to believe that God is the all-powerful and good daddy we can depend on.

6. Jesus was God's object lesson about Himself: God's live demonstration on earth.

7. God was showing Himself to us in the person of Jesus.

8. To further connect with and experience God's love, we need to have an experience of other people who love us for who we are, without conditions.

Processing Questions

1. What difficulty do you have believing in a God who is physically greater or stronger than you?

2. What questions or doubts arise for you when you think about God being good? (e.g., "What about all the suffering in the world.").

3. When is it hardest for you to believe God is all-powerful and all-good?

4. When is it especially important for you to have a God who is all-powerful and all-good?

5. Who was it that first demonstrated God's unconditional love to you?

6. How do you react when you meet someone who shows you love with no strings attached and acceptance that you don't have to earn by performing?

7. How has an unloving environment hindered you from understanding God's power and goodness?

8. Having learned something of God's unconditional love, how can you now respond to those who have been hurtful?

Characteristic God Responses

1. God is still all-powerful and all-good, even when suffering and doubt occurs.

2. God is trustworthy and dependable.

3. God's love, in Christ Jesus, is not conditional on the person's performance.

Life in Process

RENEWED SANITY
Worksheet 4

Summary Points

1. Sanity from a Christian perspective acknowledges God.

2. His position as Creator and His character as being love, are recognized.

3. A sane conclusion is that we are His dearly loved children who are to depend upon Him.

4. Insanity has to do with the way a person reacts to stressful situations, like the ones that occur when life is becoming unmanageable.

5. Insane thinking in a particular area of one's life, leads to repeated unproductive or destructive patterns — like "broken-record thinking" — the same messages keep coming up over and over.

Processing Questions

1. Briefly describe your own personal growth journey in coming to a more sane thinking about God's love.

2. Where is God when your thinking becomes insane?

Characteristic God Responses

1. As God's dearly loved child, the person can depend on him.

2. Acknowledging God and his love is a sound basis for breaking out of destructive patterns.

Life in Process

TURNING TO GOD
Worksheet 5

Summary Points

1. Turning one's life over to the management of God actually involves a series of smaller turnings.

2. As one identifies what is broken or unmanageable in one's life, then turning to God can occur.

3. A core hindrance to giving our problems over to God is distrust.

4. As one makes the move to turn to God and considers turning the unmanageableness over to God, hidden hindrances can surface.

5. There is an opportunity to look more deeply into one's self and one's past to learn what is there that still bothers or limits.

Processing Questions

1. What has "turning to God" meant to you?

2. What has God done during the times you have turned to Him?

3. What relationships or events, when remembered even now, still bother or hurt you, even though these things may have taken place long ago?

4. What do you think God wants to do with your hindrances?

Characteristic God Responses

1. God is ready to receive our unmanageableness.

2. God already knows everything about the person and fully accepts the person, so there is no need to try to hide or deny the past.

3. God loves the person and is with the person in the process of working through hindrances.

Life in Process

THE LIFE INVENTORY
Worksheet 6

Summary Points

1. There is often a resistance to remembering and looking at negative childhood events.

2. These resistances are sometimes defenses to protect us.

3. Overwhelming emotions can also cause one to retreat from taking an inventory.

4. The life inventory is a visit back to one's past.

5. A time of renewal is a time for cleansing and healing from old hurts.

6. A time of renewal is also a time to reflect on where one's life has been, both in terms of negative events, as well as the positive ones.

Processing Questions

1. What happens to you when you remember certain painful areas of your childhood?

2. Where is Jesus when you remember your past?

3. What were the following people like when you were growing up:
   Father?

   Mother?

   Describe one or two significant relatives (e.g., siblings, aunts, uncles or grandparents).

   Describe one or two people who had a major impact on you (e.g., teachers, coaches, Sunday School teachers).

4. List events (both positive and negative) that have continued to stand out in your mind, even though they occurred while you were growing up.

Characteristic God Responses

1. God understands and is patient and gracious as the person resists taking the inventory.

2. God's love is poured out into the person's heart as hurt and suffering is remembered.

3. God is always ready to reach out, forgive, and reassure of His love and acceptance.

Life in Process

ADMITTING
Worksheet 7

Summary Points

1. A true admission is a specific confession that is accompanied by godly sorrow and remorse.

2. There is not the attitude of defending oneself.

3. Underlying much of the hiding from an awareness of one's shortcomings or of having been sinned against, is a deep sense of unacceptableness.

4. As one can come to understand and then experience God's unconditional love in Christ Jesus, this sense of being unacceptable lessens.

5. God's acceptance and being seen by Him as perfect in Christ can free a person to be more honest and open.

Processing Questions

1. What admission do you need to make to yourself or others about your life?

2. How is your admission connected to the unmanageableness of your present life?

3. When did you ever feel unacceptable because your performance was less than perfect?

4. How does knowing you are fully pleasing and acceptable to God change your feelings about yourself?

Characteristic God Responses

1. No matter how bad the offence, God's unconditional love, in Christ Jesus, is always God's stance towards the person.

2. The person is encouraged, by God's constant acceptance, to be open and honest with Him and with others.

3. God continually finds ways to remind the person that his love and acceptance are not tied to the person's behavior.

Life in Process

COMMITTING AND DESIRING FOR GOD TO REMOVE PATTERNS
Worksheet 8

Summary Points

1. Trust and will are two keys to unlocking a victorious, abundant Christian life.

2. People often cling to well-worn, consistently ineffective, unhealthy, destructive, recurring patterns of living.

3. An act of will is required to move out of the pain.

4. The moving out is done as one directs the will toward trusting the person of God.

5. As dearly loved children of God, Christians have an inheritance.

6. As long as there are hindrances, the person will have difficulty experiencing the inheritance.

7. Increasing awareness of the hindrances provides the person with a choice — a choice to come to freedom in Jesus.

Processing Questions

1. When you are at a point where you want God to remove unhealthy patterns of behavior or thinking, what distrustful thoughts invade your thinking?

2. What objections do you have to using your will to decide to trust God?

3. When you think of entrusting yourself more completely to God, what feelings and thoughts come up for you?

4. When you imagine an actively involved, healthy father, who hears and understands your needs, how does it feel to know He is working to remove your unhealthy patterns of behavior and thinking?

Characteristic God Responses

1. God is trustworthy.

2. God has committed to the person permanently in adoption.

3. God is responsive to the person's requests, in a way consistent with His love and perfect wisdom.

4. God is faithful and brings about the person's spiritual maturity.

Life in Process

HUMBLY ASKING GOD TO RENEW OUR MINDS
Worksheet 9

Summary Points

1. Free will was given to created humans by God.

2. A lack of humility bent free will in the direction of sin.

3. This bent in the direction of sin originally happened with the sin of Adam and Eve.

4. A lack of humility means that the person, in some way, does not ask God.

5. A lack of humility is also imbedded in the doubts that arise when life becomes unmanageable.

6. As one feels powerless, God can also be perceived as being unable, unwilling, or not interested in helping.

Processing Questions

1. When you are living out your daily routine, how do you exercise or use your "free will"?

2. What things do you tend to do that help numb the discomfort of an unmanageable life?

3. How have you seen misperceptions of God operate in your life, especially in the unmanageable times?

4. As life becomes more unmanageable and you feel more and more powerless, at what point do you ask God to help?

5. How can you take steps to become more closely bonded with God in order for life to be more manageable?

Characteristic God Responses

1. God does not reject the person because of a lack of humility and desires that the person come to the point of humbly asking Him.

2. God uses the unmanabgeableness in a person's life to lead the person to a place of humility, in order to receive help from Him.

3. God desires and moves in the person to replace distortions with truth about Him.

4. God desires and His actions are toward having a deeper bond with the person.

Life in Process

RENEWING SICK AND SINFUL PATTERNS
Worksheet 10

Summary Points

1. People experience both being sinned against and being sinful.

2. The fallen nature is bent in the direction of choosing sickness and sin.

3. The old story contained sick and sinful patterns, but the new story is filled with hope.

4. Experiencing one's new story involves God's active participation.

5. The more one sees God as he really is, full of goodness and power, the more one can trust Him.

6. A focus on an improved relationship with God may not appear to be a very real solution to life's problems.

7. Either God is who the Bible says He is, in all His power and love, or He is not God.

8. If He is all-powerful, all-present, and all-knowing, and He loves us dearly, then our healing is very much related to Him.

Processing Questions

1. When you think about being freed from sick and sinful patterns, what is your reaction?

2. When in life have you experienced God being actively involved with you?

3. How did you feel knowing He was with you and working for you?

4. How relevant is your relationship with God when you experience life's struggles?

5. What would the effect be on your life if you could reject your doubts about God's caring for you and his actively assisting you?

Characteristic God Responses

1. God is angry with those who sinned against the person.

2. God is not put-off by the person's sick and sinful patterns.

3. God has made true healing connected to relationship with Him.

4. God doesn't abandon the person who has sick and sinful patterns, and He is active in the process of freeing the person from them.

5. God is patient with doubt that comes from being sinned against and understands the affect it has on trust.

Life in Process

TRANSFORMING INTO PATTERNS OF RIGHTEOUSNESS
Worksheet 11

Summary Points

1. There are two types of righteousness in the Christian life.

2. The first and most critical righteousness comes as an act of God when the person is saved — Jesus is then the person's righteousness.

3. Jesus did the work that provides the way for us to stand confidently before God.

4. God is able to accept us completely in Jesus, in regard to the righteousness in Jesus.

5. The other righteousness has to do with our performance.

6. Performance righteousness does not establish or maintain our status as children of God.

7. Performance righteousness does not earn God's acceptance.

8. Performance righteousness is, however, the result of our having the right relationships God desires for us to have with Himself, others, and ourselves.

9. Performance righteousness comes from being truly loved, and it is being truly loving.

10. Once one has done the psychological work of identifying old hindrances and humbly asking God to remove them, then there are fewer hindrances to growth as God works within.

11. This work brings the person into a more complete oneness with God.

Processing Questions

1. What does it mean to you to hear that God accepts you completely in Jesus?

2. When have you felt this type of unconditional acceptance in your relationships with others?

3. Being righteous in our performance means being more like Jesus. How successful have you been at living more righteously?

4. When your life feels unmanageable and you are unable to pull it all   together, how do you think God is working in you to develop your righteousness?

5. What parts of your inner person still remain separate from God?

6. How have you experienced the separate places of your heart become more one with God and your bond deeper with him?

Characteristic God Responses

1. God is actively working for the best interest of the person, in the removal of hindrances.

2. God desires that the positive work of Christ also becomes real in the person's life.

3. God desires that the person's performance comes out of gratitude not fear.

4. God pursues a deeper relationship with the person, based in His complete acceptance of the person in Christ.

Life in Process

WILLING TO AMEND
Worksheet 12

Summary Points

1. Amending is making things right with another after there has been a rift in the relationship.

2. The rift may be the result of a real or perceived offense.

3. Unwillingness to make amends is often the result of contamination of the current relationship by a past difficult relationship.

4. To be willing to amend means to be willing to take responsibility for whatever may be contaminating from one's own past.

5. One identifies what remains against the other.

6. One's own self-interest or negative defenses and motives may emerge as a further hindrance.

7. There needs to be a transcending and an overcoming of the offenses.

8. The willingness to make amends is first a turning away from the evil that can follow a conflict with another.

9. Willingness is then a turning toward one's primary relationship with God.

10. One can then admit and move toward humbly asking Him to repair first the offense with Him and then with the other.

Processing Questions

1. When you think about someone you currently have difficulties with, what traits or behaviors bother you most?

2. What person in your past, perhaps a parent, had similar traits or behaviors?

3. What is usually your initial reaction when someone hurts or offends you?

4. What negative defenses or motives are present in you at these times of being wronged?

5. What resistance to turning to God happens for you when you have been offended?

6. When your heart is right with God, how is it easier for you to forgive others?

Characteristic God Responses

1. God is with the person always.

2. God is patient and desires a turning to Him.

3. God understands the benefit that comes from being openly willing to have a right heart with Him and others.

Life in Process

AMENDING
Worksheet 13

Summary Points

1. Amending requires a person to transcend his/her own negative feelings about the other person.

2. The source of strength to love another person, in spite of the relationship failures, the fights, the hurts, is ultimately a strength that comes from the improved quality of one's deeply bonded relationship with God.

3. After going in prayer and asking for His forgiveness and assistance, it is time to go to the other person.

4. As one plans how to make your amends, remembering His deep love will make it easier to go to the other person with humility.

5. If God's great love and valuing is not remembered, pride and defensiveness will re-emerge.

Processing Questions

1. When you have something against another person, how do you experience your relationship with God?

2. How would feeling more deeply loved and accepted by God help you to make amends?

3. With whom do you need to make amends and what are the specific wrongs you have done?

4. How would feeling closely bonded with God help you love the one with whom you are making amends?

Characteristic God Responses

1. God is with the person always.

2. God is patient and desires a turning to Him.

3. God understands the benefit that comes from being openly willing to have a right heart with Him and others.

4. God is present with the person to strengthen the person in the action of amending.

Life in Process

THE INVENTORY CONTINUED AND ADMISSIONS PROMPTLY MADE
Worksheet 14

Summary Points

1. The need for a continuous inventory taking comes from the tendency for old patterns to reemerge.

2. This reemerging is not failure, nor does it indicate one is still under the old story.

3. The new story is the reality, but old tendencies can be triggered.

4. In this continuous inventory taking one must remember God's presence.

5. He is all-knowing and constantly present everywhere at the same time — an ever-present help.

6. The sense of feeling distant from God is an important indicator of the need to take inventory and to turn to Him.

Processing Questions

1. When you realize the old story, unhealthy thoughts, feelings, or behavior have re-emerged what action can you take?

2. What do you do to keep aware of your life and the old story tendencies?

3. When do you feel distant from God?

4. How does your feeling distant from God relate to slipping into your old story patterns of thinking, feeling or behaving?

Characteristic God Responses

1. God perseveres with the person and is faithful even if the person does not remain constant.

2. God has a long-term view of the person's growth toward Christlikeness.

3. God desires the person to draw near to Him, and He is not far from the person — He will never leave or forsake.

Life in Process

SEEKING GROWTH IN JESUS
Worksheet 15

Summary Points

1. Seeking growth in one's relationship with Jesus is reaching beyond the limits of this world.

2. Jesus is the "passageway to the other dimension".

3. Through Him we can reach out and come into contact with God and His kingdom.

4. To seek growth with Jesus is to seek a more deeply bonded relationship with Him.

5. To grow within a relationship is different than growing in one's knowledge of certain facts or principles — like the difference between reading a biography about a great person and living with that great person.

6. To know Jesus and to be more intimately bonded with Him moves a person beyond his/her own self-interests alone.

7. If it is understood that we are under His constant loving care, we can also realize and experience a freedom from worry.

8. Freedom from worry is a freedom that allows us to more fully attend to the purposes of God.

Processing Questions

1. How does your perspective on life change when you reflect on the spiritual reality beyond this world?

2. What do you do to keep reminded of the Kingdom of God?

3. How have you known facts or concepts about Jesus without having the experience of living with Him?

4. What difference does it make to you to know more intimately the person of Jesus and not just information about Him?

5. How would your life be different if you could trust God to take care of your needs, while you acted responsibly and mindfully in furthering the kingdom of God?

6. What do you think of a trust in God that has little regard for the worries of life and is focused on seeking God?

Characteristic God Responses

1. God has a long-term view of the person's growth toward Christlikeness.

2. God has not left the person on his/her own to grow spiritually.

3. God wants the person to not just know about Him, but to actually know Him in a continuous, personal, relational manner.

4. God wants to bear burdens with the person, because He cares for the person.

Appendix P: Life in Process Worksheets for Not-Consciously-Christian Clients

Life in Process Worksheets for Not-Consciously-Christian Clients
A NOTE TO LIFE MENTORS

The following worksheets are a revision of the *Life in Process* worksheets that were written from a specifically Christian perspective. This makes the task of revision for the "Not-Consciously-Christian" more challenging, as the content had to be changed to reflect a general "higher power" concept or at least something greater than oneself. This change is significant and removes much of the positive, personal impact and power. However, it is hoped that there is sufficient content remaining to challenge Not-Consciously-Christian individuals toward positive change. Perhaps there is also something in the process that will further their interest in the true Higher Power.

Please also keep as a consideration that this is an initial attempt at a revision. There is likely still much to be clarified and reworded. Your input will be valuable for making further revisions, and patience is asked of you as you use the current form of the worksheets. As a case in point, you will see that in the **Beliefs About Responses** worksheet section it is asking your clients to "imagine" some responses from a higher power and other people. Some clients will already have some or most of these beliefs, but others may have more difficulty with believing that these responses could happen. I would be especially interested to hear from you about how well this "imagine" approach works with your clients.

When using the worksheets, please provide them to your client one at a time. This is recommended because it may be overwhelming to receive them all at once, and you might need to consider rewording or clarifying later worksheets, due to your clients' reactions to prior ones. Additionally, your clients may not complete the full course of the life mentoring meetings with you, and if given all the worksheets, they would not have the benefit of your assistance to work through them and address content that is unclear.

I hope that your work with Not-Consciously-Christian individuals goes exceptionally and perhaps even amazingly well.

Dr. Dennis Morgan
3.October.2017
Vienna, AT

Life in Process

UNMANAGEABLENESS
Worksheet 1

Summary Points

1. Unmanageable is defined as a life that is out of control in some certain personal areas of one's life or more generally in all areas.

2. Unmanageableness can be identified by noticing areas of over-attention.

3. Unmanageableness is being demonstrated if something or someone negatively consumes large quantities of time and energy and limits the person.

4. Unmanageableness takes away from effectiveness in living.

5. Unmanageableness hinders relating with others.

6. Unmanageableness hinders use of one's higher power.

7. When life is out of control, it is difficult to manage even daily routines.

Processing Questions

1. At what point does your life seem out of control?

2. What emotions does being out of control produce in you?

3. What do you tend to do when you get to this point?

4. What advantages are there to finally "hitting bottom" and realizing life is out of control?

5. What do you think about yourself when your life is out of control

6. How does this unmanageableness affect your use of others' support?

7. How does this unmanageableness affect your use of your higher power?

8. If there are dark rooms of your life, what would it be like to become more aware of them?

Beliefs About Responses

1. Imagine what it would be like to have a higher power and other people who can see and understand another's unmanageableness.

2. Imagine the experience of a higher power and other people whose love would be extended to others even while their lives seem out of control.

3. The unmanageableness blocks your experience of the care and concern of others.

4. The unmanageableness blocks your experience of a higher power.

5. Imagine what it would be like if a higher power and other people wanted to be actively involved and wanted to help a person with the unmanageableness, even if the person didn't believe that they would.

Life in Process

POWERLESSNESS
Worksheet 2

Summary Points

1. When we find that our lives are unmanageable in some areas, we're faced with what to do about it.

2. The result is that we may try many ways to cope.

3. Here are some typical ways people try to cope, but they are not true solutions.

Drug/alcohol addiction	Dependency on others
Overeating	Focusing on helping others
Working too hard	Controlling others
Numbing out	

4. We are powerless to control everything that happens to us — to change every life circumstance.

5. We are to some extent forced to depend on other people and other things.

6. Dependence must be approached carefully. No other person is safe enough and powerful enough to handle our complete dependence.

7. No thing (e.g., money, possessions, drugs, etc.) can rightfully be an object of our ultimate trust.

8. Negative feelings about being dependent are common, especially for those who have experienced being hurt while depending on others.

9. Being dependent itself is not harmful when we depend appropriately upon someone safe.

10. One could try to imagine what it would be like to have someone perfectly reliable to depend on, such as a higher power.

11. Being powerless is a condition of being human, because there are areas of our lives where we cannot manage completely on our own — not having the needed resources or power.

12. Because it is a common human desire, we can understand this need to depend on someone who is fully trustworthy.

13. While we move toward depending more on a Higher Power or someone safe and trustworthy, there are other people and things that we are tempted to misuse against the powerlessness.

14. The situation is one of being powerless (i.e., not all-powerful) and in need of finding appropriate ways to be dependent.

Processing Questions

1. Where have you recognized powerlessness in your own life?

2. What emotional responses do you encounter when you personally confront your own powerlessness?

3. What things have you used to maintain the feeling of power and deny powerlessness?

4. What healthy ways have you learned to express your dependency in a time of need?

5. In what areas do you have difficulty depending on your Higher Power or others for help?

Beliefs About Responses

1. It is important to become aware of the negative ways that one tries in order to cope with powerlessness.

2. Imagine how being gracious and patient with yourself, throughout the process of coping, could improve your resilience.

3. Though we can never be certain that another will never let us down, imagine what it would be like if there were people to whom one could safely turn to in a time of need.

4. Imagine how a higher power outside of oneself, could be helpful in admitting one's own limitations.

Life in Process

BELIEF IN SOMEONE OR SOMETHING GREATER THAN MYSELF
Worksheet 3

Summary Points

1. Belief in someone or something greater than ourselves (a higher power) has various aspects.

2. Would this someone or something be more powerful in the sense of physical strength?

3. The greater than ourselves also applies to character qualities of this someone or something, e.g., powerfulness and goodness.

4. Doubts about this someone or something's power and goodness (and being loving) would undermine trust.

5. When doubt is present, it is difficult to believe that this someone or something can be depended on.

6. To further connect with and experience this someone or something's love, we need to have had, in our personal history, a human experience of other people who have loved us for who we are, without conditions of performance.

Processing Questions

1. What difficulty do you have believing in this someone or something who is significantly physically greater or stronger than you?

2. What questions or doubts arise for you when you think about a higher power being good? (e.g., "What about all the suffering in the world.").

3. When is it hardest for you to believe in someone or something who is this powerful and good?

4. When is it especially important for you to have this someone or something who is powerful and good?

5. Who was it that first demonstrated unconditional love to you?

6. How do you react when you meet someone who shows you love with no strings attached and acceptance that you don't have to earn by performing?

7. How has an unloving environment hindered you from understanding someone or something's power and goodness?

8. Having learned something of a higher power's unconditional love, how would you then respond to those who have been hurtful?

Beliefs About Responses

1. Imagine the experience of there being someone or something who would still be powerful and good, even when your suffering occurs and causes you to doubt.

2. Imagine the experience of knowing someone or something (higher power) who is trustworthy and dependable.

3. Imagine what it would be like to have a higher power whose love would not be conditional on your performance.

Life in Process

RENEWED SANITY
Worksheet 4

Summary Points

1. Sanity from this spiritual perspective acknowledges a higher power.

2. The qualities and operation of the higher power are recognized.

3. A sane conclusion is that we need reference points, from a higher power and other people, in order to keep our perspective in life.

4. Insanity has to do with the way a person reacts to stressful situations, like the ones that occur when life is becoming unmanageable.

5. Insane thinking in a particular area of one's life leads to repeated unproductive or destructive patterns — like "broken-record thinking" — the same messages keep coming up over and over.

Processing Questions

1. Briefly describe your own personal journey in experiencing and accessing a higher power or something beyond yourself.

2. How helpful or unhelpful is your higher power when your thinking becomes insane?

Beliefs About Responses

1. Since people can never fully depend solely on themselves or others, due to human limitations, imagine what it would be like to utilize a higher power as a further resource for being able to change.

2. Imagine the experience of acknowledging the need for assistance, from others and from one's higher power, in order to be able to break out of destructive patterns in life.

Life in Process

TURNING TO SOMEONE OR SOMETHING GREATER
Worksheet 5

Summary Points

1. Incorporating a higher power's assistance for living better, overall, involves a series of smaller turnings to or enlisting of one's higher power.

2. As one identifies what is broken or unmanageable in one's life, then turning to a higher power can occur.

3. A core hindrance to giving our problems over to a higher power is distrust.

4. As one considers turning to a higher power to assist with the unmanageableness, hidden hindrances can surface.

5. There is an opportunity to look more deeply into oneself and one's past to learn what is there that still bothers or limits.

Processing Questions

1. What does "turning to a higher power" mean to you?

2. What has your higher power provided for you when you have turned to it for assistance?

3. What relationships or events, when remembered even now, still bother or hurt you, even though these things may have taken place long ago?

4. When it comes to reducing the things that hinder you, how do you think that having a higher power would help?

Beliefs About Responses

1. Imagine that there are is a higher power and there are other people too who are safe enough to be trusted.

2. Imagine disclosing deeper personal things to a trusted other person and experiencing that the other person still fully accepts you, which is freeing and encouraging of further trust and openness.

3. Imagine a trusted other person who can "walk" with you in the process of working through hindrances.

Life in Process

THE LIFE INVENTORY
Worksheet 6

Summary Points

1. There is often a resistance to remembering and looking at negative childhood events.

2. These resistances are sometimes defenses to protect us.

3. Overwhelming emotions can also cause one to retreat from taking an inventory.

4. The life inventory is a visit back to one's past.

5. A time of renewal is a time for cleansing and healing from old hurts.

6. A time of renewal is also a time to reflect on where one's life has been, both in terms of negative events, as well as the positive ones.

Processing Questions

1. What happens to you when you remember certain painful areas of your childhood?

2. How is or could your higher power be involved when you remember your past?

3. What were the following people like when you were growing up:
   Father?

Mother?

Describe one or two significant relatives (e.g., siblings, aunts, uncles or grandparents).

Describe one or two people who had a major impact on you (e.g., teachers, coaches, neighbors).

4. List events (both positive and negative) that have continued to stand out in your mind, even though they occurred while you were growing up.

Beliefs About Responses

1. Imagine what it would be like for there to be others who are willing to understand and be patient and gracious as a person resists taking the inventory.

2. Imagine the experience of someone who can trust others with personal information of past hurt and suffering, and while disclosing this, is being responded to with comforting support.

3. Imagine further what it would be like for you if trusted individuals could be expected to reach out to you and forgive and reassure you of their love and acceptance.

4. Imagine how it would be to experience a higher power also supplying the encouragement to face the past and go forward positively in life.

Life in Process

ADMITTING
Worksheet 7

Summary Points

1. A true admission is a specific confession that is accompanied by sorrow and remorse for hurting others.

2. There is not the attitude of defending oneself.

3. Underlying much of the hiding from awareness of one's shortcomings or of having been sinned against, is a deep sense of unacceptableness.

4. As one can come to understand and then experience love from others that is free from judgment and expectations, the sense of being unacceptable lessens.

5. Feelings of acceptance and being seen by others as acceptable, can free a person to be more honest and open.

Processing Questions

1. What admission do you need to make to yourself or others about your life?

2. How is your admission connected to the unmanageableness of your present life?

3. When did you ever feel unacceptable because your performance was less than perfect?

4. How would knowing you are fully loved and accepted by another person change your feelings about yourself?

5. How does your higher power further enable you to admit to others?

Beliefs About Responses

1. Imagine what it would be like to know that no matter how bad the offence, there are people capable of continued love and acceptance towards you.

2. Imagine the experience of a person who has constant acceptance from another individual and whose courage is strengthened to become more open and honest with others.

3. Imagine how it would be to have a consistent love and acceptance from others who also demonstrate that love and acceptance are not dependent on good behavior or performance.

4. Imagine experiencing a higher power who is offering an unconditional love that is not dependent on performance.

Life in Process

COMMITTING AND DESIRING FOR PATTERNS TO BE REMOVED
Worksheet 8

Summary Points

1. Trust and will are two important ingredients for flourishing in life.

2. People often cling to well-worn, consistently ineffective, unhealthy, destructive, recurring patterns of living.

3. An act of will is required to move out of the pain.

4. The moving-out is done as one relies on trusted friends, along with one's higher power, while also directing the will toward change.

5. As long as there are hindrances, the person will have difficulty flourishing in life.

6. Increasing awareness of the hindrances provides the person with a choice — a choice to move toward healthy patterns in living.

Processing Questions

1. When you want to remove unhealthy patterns of behavior or thinking, what distrustful thoughts invade your thinking?

2. What objections do you have to using your will to decide to trust a higher power or someone else?

3. When you think of entrusting yourself more completely to another person or to your higher power, what feelings and thoughts come up for you?

4. When you imagine an actively involved, healthy person or higher power, who hears and understands your needs, how does it feel to know that person or power is working to help you remove your unhealthy patterns of behavior and thinking?

Beliefs About Responses

1. Imagine what it would be to like have relationships with others who are trustworthy and can be counted on.

2. Imagine experiencing a relationship with a healthy, trustworthy friend who can provide good input into your life.

Life in Process

HUMBLY ASKING FOR A RENEWAL OF OUR MINDS
Worksheet 9

Summary Points

1. Humans have a freedom of their wills that allows choice, sometimes termed "free will".

2. A lack of humility bends choice in a negative direction.

3. This bent in humans toward a negative direction has a long history in mankind.

4. A lack of humility means that the person, in some way, does not ask for change.

5. A lack of humility is also imbedded in the doubts that arise when life becomes unmanageable — for example, too proud to ask for help.

6. As one feels powerless, a higher power can also be perceived as being unable, unwilling, or not interested in helping.

Processing Questions

1. When you are living out your daily routine, how do you exercise or use your "free will"?

2. What things do you tend to do that help numb the discomfort of an unmanageable life?

3. How have you seen misperceptions about others operate in your life, especially in the unmanageable times — for example having distrustful thoughts?

4. As life becomes more unmanageable and you feel more and more powerless, at what point do you ask for help?

5. How can you take steps to become more closely bonded with others and/or a higher power, in order for life to be more manageable?

Beliefs About Responses

1. Imagine how it would be to have a higher power who does not reject a person because of a lack of humility and desires that the person comes to the point of humbly asking for help.

2. Imagine what it would be like to have a higher power who uses the unmanageableness in a person's life to lead the person to a place of humility, in order to be more ready to receive help.

3. Imagine the experience of having a higher power who desires to assist a person to replace distorted thinking with truth.

4. Image what it would be like to have a higher power who wants to have a deeper bond with you and acts accordingly toward having that deeper bond.

Life in Process

RENEWING DYSFUNCTIONAL PATTERNS
Worksheet 10

Summary Points

1. People experience both being mistreated, as well as mistreating others.

2. Though humans are capable of achieving great things, human nature also has bent in the direction of choosing dysfunction and sometimes that which is evil.

3. The old story in our lives contained dysfunctional patterns, but there can be a new story that is filled with hope.

4. Experiencing one's new story can be enhanced through the active involvement of a higher power.

5. The more one perceives this higher power as being full of goodness and power, the more one can trust.

6. A focus on increasing reliance on a higher power may not appear to be a real or direct type of solution to life's problems.

7. If one's higher power is powerful enough, is available, and is benevolent, then the healing process can very much include this higher power.

Processing Questions

1. When you think about being freed from dysfunctional patterns, what is your reaction?

2. When in life have you experienced a higher power being actively involved with you?

3. How did you feel knowing that your higher power was with you and working for you?

4. How relevant is your relationship with a higher power when you are experiencing life's struggles?

5. What would the effect be on your life if you could reject your doubts about your higher power's care for you and it's active assistance?

Beliefs About Responses

1. Imagine how it would be to have a higher power who is angry with those who mistreat others.

2. Imagine what it would be like to be in a relationship with a higher power who is not put-off by the person's dysfunctional patterns.

3. Imagine experiencing a relationship with a higher power that facilitates healing.

4. Imagine the experience of having a higher power who does not abandon you in the dysfunctional patterns and is active in the process of freeing you from them.

5. Imagine what it would be like to have a higher power who is patient with the doubt that comes from being mistreated by others and understands the negative affect that mistreatment has on trust.

Life in Process

TRANSFORMING INTO PATTERNS OF RIGHTNESS
Worksheet 11

Summary Points

1. There is a type of being made right (to be put back into a positive relationship with) that is external, as in forgiveness or a judge's pardon. There is a becoming more right (more healthy and functional) that is internal, as in positive personal character strengthening and growth.

2. Both types of rightness also bring peace, both with others and within one's self.

3. A higher power who accepts us completely and unconditionally would offer more security as we work on becoming more right within ourselves and with others.

4. There is a kind of love, an unconditional love, that covers the other person's imperfections (considers others as all-right) and is a gift, not based on performance.

5. Performance-based seeking of rightness or approval is not the foundation of an unconditional love.

6. Performance-based rightness is not needed to earn an unconditionally loving higher power's acceptance — it is a gift.

7. Performance rightness (right responses) follows or results from our having already been made right in relationship to ourselves and others.

8. Performance rightness flows from already being unconditionally loved, and then becomes being unconditionally loving toward others.

9. Once one has done the psychological work of identifying old dysfunctional patterns and has asked for assistance in removing them, the desired result is that there are fewer hindrances to continued growth.

10. This progressive positive change process brings the person into a closer relationship with one's higher power and with others.

Processing Questions

1. What does it mean to you to know that you are accepted completely and unconditionally by someone?

2. When have you felt this type of unconditional acceptance in your relationships with others?

3. Being right in our performance means being more functional and healthy. How successful have you been at living more rightly?

4. When your life feels unmanageable and you are unable to pull it all together, how do you think your higher power is working in you to develop your rightness?

5. What parts of yourself still remain in internal conflict?

6. How have you experienced the parts of yourself more at peace internally and in your connections with your higher power and others?

Beliefs About Responses

1. Imagine what it would be like to have a higher power who is actively working for your best interest in helping you to be more right.

2. Imagine how it would be to know your higher power desires that this positive work becomes more real in your experience of life.

3. Imagine what it would be like to know your higher power desires that your performance comes out of gratitude not fear.

4. Imagine the experience of knowing that your higher power is wanting a deeper relationship with you — one that is based on unconditional love.

Life in Process

WILLING TO AMEND
Worksheet 12

Summary Points

1. Amending is making things right with another after there has been a rift in the relationship.

2. The rift may be the result of a real or perceived offense.

3. Unwillingness to make amends is often the result of contamination of the current relationship by a past difficult relationship.

4. To be willing to amend means to be willing to take responsibility for whatever may be contaminating from one's own past.

5. One identifies what remains against the other.

6. One's own self-interest or negative defenses and motives may emerge as a further hindrance.

7. There needs to be a transcending and an overcoming of the offenses.

8. The willingness to make amends is first a turning away from the evil that can follow a conflict with another.

9. Willingness is then enhanced by turning toward one's higher power.

10. One can then admit and move toward humbly asking one's higher power for assistance with repairing relationships.

Processing Questions

1. When you think about someone you currently have difficulties with, what traits or behaviors bother you most?

2. What person in your past, perhaps a parent, had similar traits or behaviors?

3. What is usually your initial reaction when someone hurts or offends you?

4. What negative defenses or motives are present in you at these times of being wronged?

5. What resistance to turning to your higher power might happen when you have been offended?

6. When your heart is right (e.g., by being at peace), how is it made easier for you to forgive others?

Beliefs About Responses

1. Imagine what it would be like if a higher power is with you always.

2. Imagine the experience of having a higher power who is patient and desires to be turned-to for assistance.

3. Imagine how it would be to have a higher power who understands the benefit that comes from being open and willing to repair relationships with others.

Life in Process

AMENDING
Worksheet 13

Summary Points

1. Amending requires a person to transcend his/her own negative feelings about the other person.

2. A source of strength to love another person, in spite of the relationship failures, the fights, the hurts, can come from an improved quality of relationship with one's higher power.

3. After going to one's higher power and asking for assistance, it is then time to go to the other person.

4. As one plans how to make amends, remembering the unconditional love of one's higher power will make it easier to go to the other person with humility.

5. If the love and valuing of one's higher power is not remembered, then pride and defensiveness may more easily re-emerge.

Processing Questions

1. When you have something against another person, how do you experience your relationship with your higher power as helping?

2. How would feeling more unconditionally loved and accepted by your higher power help you to make amends?

3. With whom do you need to make amends and what are the specific wrongs you have done?

4. How would feeling a close bond with your higher power help you love the one with whom you are making amends?

Beliefs About Responses

1. Imagine the experience of having a higher power who is with you always.

2. Imagine again what it would be like to have a higher power who is patient and desires to be of assistance.

3. Imagine again how it would be for a higher power to understand the benefit that comes from being openly willing to have a right relationship with others.

4. Imagine the experience of having a higher power who is present with you to strengthen you in taking the action of making amends with another.

Life in Process

THE INVENTORY CONTINUED AND ADMISSIONS PROMPTLY MADE
Worksheet 14

Summary Points

1. The need for a continuous inventory taking comes from the tendency for old patterns to re-emerge.

2. This re-emerging is not failure, nor does it indicate one is still under the old story.

3. The new story is the reality, but old tendencies can be triggered.

4. In this continuous inventory taking there is benefit in remembering the presence of one's higher power.

5. A more affective higher power is one who is an ever-present help/resource.

6. The sense of feeling distant from a higher power may be an important indicator of the need to take inventory.

Processing Questions

1. When you realize the old story, unhealthy thoughts, feelings, or behavior have re-emerged what action can you take?

2. What do you do to keep aware of your life and the old story tendencies?

3. When do you feel distant from your higher power?

4. How does your feeling distant from your higher power relate to slipping into your old story patterns of thinking, feeling or behaving?

Beliefs About Responses

1. Imagine the experience of knowing that a higher power perseveres with you and is faithful to you even if you don't remain constant.

2. Imagine what it would be like to have a higher power who has a long-term view of your growth toward strengthened character and resilience.

3. Imagine experiencing a higher power who desires you to draw near to you, is never far from you, and is always available for you.

Life in Process

SEEKING GROWTH
Worksheet 15

Summary Points

1. Seeking growth in one's relationship with others is reaching beyond the limits of ourselves.

2. A mentor can provide a model for us to imitate.

3. To seek growth in relationships with others is to seek to become more bonded and emotionally intimate with others.

4. To grow within a relationship is different than growing in one's knowledge of certain facts or principles — like the difference between reading a biography about a great person and living with that great person.

5. To know more fully and to be more intimately bonded with others moves a person beyond his/her own self-interests alone.

6. If it is understood that we are unconditionally loved by another, then we can also realize and experience a freedom from concern about being acceptable.

7. Freedom from this concern about acceptance frees us to be more transparent with trusted others.

Processing Questions

1. How could your perspective on life change if you reflected on a spiritual reality or higher power beyond this world?

2. What could you do to keep reminded of this spiritual reality?

3. If you know about or have a higher power, what has that experience been like?

4. What difference would it make to you to know a higher power more personally and not just as information or facts?

5. How would your life be different if you could trust a higher power to take care of your needs, while you acted responsibly?

6. What do you think of a trust in a higher power that has little regard for the worries of life and is focused on seeking this higher power?

Beliefs About Responses

1. Imagine what it would be like to know that others and a higher power have a long-term view of your growth in character strengths.

2. Imagine the experience of having others and a higher power who would be there for you, and you would not be left on your own to grow personally and spiritually.

3. Imagine experiencing a relationship with a higher power who wants a personal relationship with you — to not just know facts about you, but to actually know you in a continuous, personal, relational manner.

4. Imagine what it would be like to have a higher power who wants to bear burdens with you, because of caring for you.

ENDNOTES

Endnotes

I   Morgan, *Person and Character Level Life Coaching and Mentoring.*

II.   GriefShare is a grief recovery support group where people can find help and healing for the hurt of losing a loved one: www.griefshare.org.

III.   Hubble, *Heart and Soul of Change.* The first chapter on empirical foundations can be understood as a further explanation of the conclusion that psychotherapy outcome variance is attributable to the following factors in discernible proportions:

- 40%: client and extra-therapeutic factors (such as ego strength, social support, etc.)
- 30%: therapeutic relationship (such as empathy, warmth, and encouragement of risk taking)
- 15%: expectancy and placebo effects
- 15%: techniques unique to specific therapies.

IV.   As you read though this book or its prior companion book, you may wonder why more is not said about resilience. Resilience is listed as one of the three Life Goals in the Person and Character Level (PCL) life mentoring and life coaching model of change, so why is resilience not explained more fully and incorporated more explicitly into the PCL model-of-change material?

There is a reason for placing improved personal coping and resilience third and last in the list of Life Goals. Resilience is considered, in the PCL model, as primarily being a naturally resulting outcome of meeting the first two Life Goals. The improved personal coping and resilience is therefore regarded as being brought about through a strengthened here and now relationship with God (the first Life Goal) and growth in character (the second Life Goal), as these two are integrated with the situational goals and actions process of change. In other words, as important as resilience is, it is nonetheless understood to actually be a byproduct of the other important developments in the person. Resilience is being indirectly attained and achieved through the process of change, inclusive of the strengthening of character virtues and enhancement to the quality of here-and-now intimacy with God (or for the Not-Consciously-Christian, by a more immediately relevant and utilized higher power concept).

With that contextual explanation in mind, it is nevertheless important to also provide some clarification of what is meant by the term resilience and how it is connected to the change process in life mentoring and life coaching. Southwick & Charney, Resilience: The Science of Mastering Life's Greatest Challenges, 7, offer a definition of resilience.

> What is Resilience? In the physical sciences, materials and objects are termed resilient if they resume their original shape upon being bent or stretched. In people, resilience refers to the ability to "bounce back" after encountering difficulty. The American Psychological Association defines it as "the process of adapting well in the face of adversity, trauma, tragedy, threats and even significant sources of stress – such as family and relationship problems, serious health problems, or workplace and financial stresses." Harvard University psychologist George Vaillant ... describes resilient individuals as resembling "a twig with a fresh, green living core. When twisted out of shape, such a twig bends, but it does not break; instead it springs back and continues growing..."

Southwick and Charney go on to report on the research they conducted through the use of structured, in-depth interviews with resilient individuals. In this research, they found recurring themes, which they determined to be similar coping strategies across individuals. They conducted a detailed analysis and identified ten coping mechanisms that were effective in dealing with stress and trauma. They refer to these coping mechanisms as "resilience factors." The ten resilience factors they identified are: *realistic optimism, facing fear, moral compass, religion and spirituality, social support, resilient role models, physical fitness, brain fitness, cognitive and emotional flexibility, and meaning and purpose.*

Logical connections can be made between these resilience factors and the principles put forth in the PCL model of change. In particular, some of the resilience factors can also be understood as directly reflective of character strengths. That is, character strengths are understood to be necessary for appropriate and resilient reactions to situations. This is the case, for example, with the character strength of courage and the resilience factor of *facing fear.*

There are resilience factors that are connected with the PCL model's emphasis on the quality of the relationship between a helper and a client, as the helper is being a *resilient role model* and *source of social support.* In terms of relationship with God, the quality of one's spirituality is improved with the strengthening of the here and now experience of in one's relationship with Him. This strengthened here and now relationship with God would be seen as being associated with the resilience factors of having: a *moral compass, religion and spirituality, and meaning and purpose.*

The PCL model's grounding of its understanding of human nature in the view that the person is the immaterial soul and that the person is not located in the brain, is relevant as well. With the person being distinct from the brain and therefore being self-distanced from brain functioning in actuality, there is a probable advantage for improvement in the resilience factors of *brain fitness* and *cognitive and emotional flexibility.*

Additionally, in talking about the ways to enhance resilience factors, Southwick and Charney (Southwick & Charney, *Resilience: The Science of Mastering Life's Greatest* Challenges) are assuming that people have the internal ability to observe their responses and to make choices. In the PCL model, this internal ability is located in the immaterial person (the soul or spirit) — the real person. The PCL model clarifies that this soul-person is the one who has agency over the brain functioning — being able to self-distance from and have efficacy over the material brain's functioning, as well as being is capable of directing choices that are carried-out through the material brain and body. In this sense, it is the soul-person who moves the whole person toward enhanced resilience factors.

Resilience, as a concept, is not developed and elaborated in the PCL Life Coaching and Mentoring material because it is not being worked on directly. Rather, the improved personal coping and resilience is viewed as being a byproduct of other PCL positive change. However, as can be seen, the goals and actions that are incorporated into the PCL model are clearly connected with and supportive of the enhancement of the ten factors that Southwick and Charney describe as being associated with improved resilience.

V.   Morgan, *Life in Process.*

VI.   GriefShare is a grief recovery support group where people can find help and healing for the hurt of losing a loved one: www.griefshare.org.

VII.   Just as there is the real person and there is also the concept of self, there is the true God and there is the individual's concept of God. In PCL Life Mentoring and Coaching, there is an emphasis on building a conceptual and experiential bridge to God and his true character.

A concept of God is one's cognitive understanding of God. It is closely associated with one's theology. Lawrence, "Measuring the Image of God: The God Image Inventory and the God Image Scales". A related concept is one's image of God. This can be defined as one's experiential understanding and is thought to develop primarily through what a child experiences with primary care givers, such as parents. Rizzuto, *The Birth of the Living God: A Psychoanalytic Study.* (The term "image of God" as used in this context is not the same concept as when referring to humans being created in God's image.) God's true identity is filtered through the individual's concept and image of Him.

In PCL Life Mentoring and Coaching, one of the Life Goals is to improve and strengthen the person's here and now relationship with God. One can easily see the connection between this improvement and both the concept and image the person has of God. It is assumed that the process of having an increasing sense of God's positive here and now presence and involvement in one's life can necessitate changes to both one's concept and one's image of God.

Some past research has been done that relates changes in God image to material also used in PCL Life Mentoring. The Morgan, *Life in Process* book is the basis for the PCL Life Mentoring worksheets. Content from this book was also used in a dissertation study. O'Hare, *Challenging God Images: Implementing a Christian Component Within a Standard Group Therapy Intervention,* 3. A relevant outcome from this was that post-test correlations between spiritual well-being (SWB) and God image (GI) were positive and significant. In other words, using the *Life in Process* material in the group therapy, subjects improved significantly both in their spiritual well-being and in their God image.

Another way of describing the strength of one's relationship with God is to consider the type and extent of attachment the person has with God. This attachment is a corollary to the type of God concept and image the individual has.

Beck and McDonald's research was into the development of an inventory to examine the idea that relationship with God can be fruitfully described as an attachment bond. Beck and McDonald, "Attachment to God: The Attachment to God Inventory, Tests of Working Model Correspondence, and an Exploration of Faith Group Differences," 92. They state that:

> In describing the attachment bond, Ainsworth (1985) delineated four criteria: Maintaining proximity with the attachment figure, seeing the attachment figure as a secure base of explorative behavior, considering the attachment figure as providing a haven of safety, and experiencing separation anxiety when removed from the attachment figure (leading to grief if the attachment figure is also lost). Using these criteria, Kirkpatrick (1999) has persuasively argued that relationship with God can be described as an attachment bond.

For Christians, there is assurance of God's love and acceptance in Christ and there is already true acceptability because of the regeneration of the new person, now perfect in Christ. God is a safe object with whom to attach or bond. For the Not-Consciously-Christian there is the opportunity to begin to or further imagine what relationship would be like with this kind of loving and actively involved God. However, at every point in the PCL Life Mentoring or Life Coaching, it is appreciated that more extensive renewal and repair may be needed psychologically, thus necessitating a referral for professional counseling or psychotherapy.

VIII.   The psychological process known as self-distancing or psychological distancing has been defined as, "...a process in which peoples' direct egocentric experience of a stimulus in the here and now is diminished." Kross and Ayduk, *From a Distance: Implications of Spontaneous Self-Distancing For Adaptive Self-reflection*, 2.

Research has been done across various areas, suggesting the importance of this construct for self-control and adaptive coping. The construct of psychological self-distancing also figures prominently into clinical research, theory, and practice. "For example, Alford and Beck (1998, p. 142) wrote, 'Distancing refers to the ability to view one's own thoughts (or beliefs) as constructions of [reality] rather than as reality itself' and identified this process as an important precondition for enabling effective cognitive therapy." Ibid., 3.

In the language of the PCL Life Mentoring and Life Coaching approach, the soul-person, because of being distinct from the brain and its functioning, is able to pull away from the brain-based immersed perspective on the self-relevant events and emotions. The naturally distinct and detached soul-person can analyze negative feelings from a self-distanced perspective — a self-distanced and distinct perspective, but not completely separate from the brain-based immersed position of a recalled experience. The soul-person and brain are both within the whole person, are connected, and the soul-person has determinative influence on the brain-based psychological functioning.

Kross, *When the Self Becomes Other Toward an Integrative Understanding of the Processes Distinguishing Adaptive Self-reflection from Rumination*, 39. Kross states that, "The main goals of this paper were to shed light on why people's attempts to analyze and 'work through' negative feelings fail, and to demonstrate how such failures can be overcome by adopting a self-distanced perspective when analyzing negative events rather than a self-immersed perspective."

Ibid., 36. Kross explains that:

> Prior research indicates that when people recall negative emotional events, they typically do so from a self-immersed perspective. From this perspective, self-relevant events and emotions are experienced in the first person, through one's own eyes. However, experiences can also be focused on from a self-distanced perspective in which the individual becomes an observer of the self.... In prior research, Kross, Ayduk, and Mischel [Kross, Ayduk, and Mischel, "*When asking 'why' does not hurt: Distinguishing rumination from reflective processing of negative emotions.*"] proposed that whether people adopt a self-immersed versus self-distanced perspective would critically influence their ability to analyze negative experiences adaptively. They predicted that when individuals focus on negative feelings from a self-immersed perspective, episodic information concerning the specific chain of events (i.e., what happened) and emotions experienced (i.e., what did I feel?) would become accessible, serving to increase negative affect. In contrast, they predicted that analyzing negative feelings from a self-distanced perspective would lead people to focus less on the episodic features of their recalled experience and more on reconstruing it in ways that promote insight

and closure. In turn, they predicted that this shift in the content of people's thoughts about their past experience — less recounting and more reconstruing — would lead to reductions in negative affect.

Kross, *When the Self Becomes Other Toward an Integrative Understanding of the Processes Distinguishing Adaptive Self-Reflection from Rumination*, 36. To test these predictions, Kross and colleagues recruited subjects for a study on memory and language. "Participants were first instructed to recall a specific time from their past in which they felt overwhelming feelings of anger and hostility. They were then randomly assigned to analyze their feelings from either a self-immersed or self--distanced perspective."

> The results indicated that participants in the self-distanced group displayed significantly lower levels of emotional reactivity compared to participants in the self-immersed group. In addition, analyses of participants' thought content essays indicated that participants who analyzed their feelings from a self-distanced perspective focused relatively less on what happened to them (i.e., recounting) and relatively more on reconstruing the event (e.g., I understand why the fight happened; it might have been irrational, but I understand his motivation now). Consistent with the experimenters' predictions, this shift in the content of people's thoughts about their past experience — less recounting and more reconstruing — mediated the effect of the self-perspective manipulations on emotional reactivity.

Self-Distancing is an important concept and tool for both PCL Life Mentoring and Life Coaching. Starting with the PCL view that humans have a non-material soul that is their person, provides a structural basis for there being the internal capacity to put oneself in a juxtaposed position to observe, assess, and act upon internal psychological processes of the material brain. In other words, by affirming that clients' persons are not their brains, the self-distancing concept is further strengthened. It is a real, distinct soul-person who has functional agency or control over brain processes. By contrast, it would appear to be a logical contradiction to say that the one-and-the-same brain is capable of both being immersed and being able to self-distance at the same time and in the same sense. For example, it is a logical contradiction to say that a man is a bachelor and a married man at the same time and in the same sense. Likewise, it would be a logical contradiction to say that the brain is an observed object and an observing agent at the same time and in the same sense of brain functioning processes.

The psychological construct of a brain-based, conscious, experiencing "self" is challengeable on philosophical grounds. Chalmers, *Facing Up to the Problem of Consciousness*, discussed this some time ago in terms of the easy problem and the hard problem with explaining consciousness. The easy problem can be handled by neuroscience in discovering the location and action of the brain when doing various functions and processes. The really hard problem is the problem of experience — the subjective aspect. Solving the easy problem does not account for the consciousness and experiencing of a self. In other words, solving the easy problem does not support that there is a brain-based "self" who unites all the various states of experience and makes them feel like something.

In more recent times, the challenge to the construct of a brain-based "self" has also come from within psychology. One example of this challenge can be found in Klein & Gangi, *The Multiplicity of Self: Neuropsychological Evidence and Its Implications for the Self as a Construct in Psychological Research*. They state that the difficulty in describing the "self" is that there may not be a *single* thing to be described. They further state that research indicates rather that the self is a multiplicity of related, yet separable, processes and contents. They argue, in their paper, that the idea that there is a "self" to be found is based on a false premise that there is a "self to be found." Instead, they attempt to show that the self consists in a collection of contents, aspects, and functions. They believe that it is no wonder that attempts to localize the self via imaging have been discouraging. Their report, interestingly, also adds that there is a growing body of evidence demonstrating that some components of the self can be profoundly damaged while others are spared, but across cases the trait "self-knowledge" (i.e., reliable knowledge of one's own personality traits) has been preserved in the face of impairments. Their conclusion is that this self-knowledge system is the most resilient in the face of cognitive chaos resulting from damage to the brain. Perhaps this self-knowledge system is actually related to someone within the whole person — the soul-person — who utilizes the brain and yet is not structurally located in the brain.

These are examples of philosophical and neuroscience challenges to the construct of brain-based explanations for an experiencing unified self. They are, I believe, consistent with the view that the immaterial soul is the person, not the brain-based "self." With this in mind, the following conclusions are put forth:

- The soul-person is the real and only person in the whole person
- The psychological "self" is a construct on-the-one-hand for convenience of explanation, but on-the-other-hand offers a faulty anthropology, because this "self" is not a person
- The psychological "self" is actually more an integrated system of brain-based memories, beliefs, processes, etc. that contributes to what would be categorized as psychological personality and its functioning
- The psychological "self" is not an entity — it is not a thing that could have awareness that the soul-person is real, and so cannot validate a belief in the soul-person by experience
- In other words, the psychological "self," not having personhood, has no independent ability to observe the soul-person, as from an outside perspective
- The soul-person is aware of, can observe, and has agency over the psychological "self"
- The psychological "self" has a kind of self-reflection, but only as animated by the soul-person
- The soul-person has conscious self-awareness and experiences, but there is no other observer perspective to affirm the soul-person existence — there is no other internal entity, in the whole person, to observe the soul-person from a perspective outside the soul-person.

Accepting that there is this immaterial soul-person goes against a metaphysical materialistic position. I believe it is fully acceptable, however, to start with the tenant that there are both immaterial as well as material things. By contrast, according to Adler, to start with the metaphysical materialist position, of a denial of the immaterial, is a negative and weak position. And even with that denial, a concession to some immaterial aspects is still required. Adler, *Intellect: Mind Over Matter*, X.

> The fundamental tenet of metaphysical materialism is that only material things exist — only physical bodies or quanta of physical energy. Nothing immaterial — nothing nonphysical or incorporeal — exists, though some physical things or processes may have aspects that appear to be immaterial.

Metaphysical materialism, stated in these bold terms, has two obvious defects. The first is that it has its foundation in a negative proposition that has never been proved and never can be. In other words, it rests on the unprovable postulate or assumption that nothing immaterial does or can exist. That assumption may be true. Making it is not an error. Asserting it dogmatically as an established truth, however, not as something that may be assumed, *is* a serious error, a culpable mistake to be avoided.

The second defect of metaphysical materialism is its grudging admission that some bodily states and physical processes have immaterial aspects....the materialist is compelled to admit that brain states and processes, which are material existences, do have what must be regarded as immaterial aspects to which we cannot help referring when we talk to one another about our conscious experiences.

Our own first-person account confirms to us that we are more than brain functions. It feels like something to be consciously aware of things and of our existence. The common response, and I believe consensus, if people are asked if they are a person apart from brain and body, would be to affirm that they experience life from this perspective.

Beyond the arguments for having an immaterial soul-person, is the acceptance based on faith. For those who are believers in the divinity, bodily existence, and resurrection of Jesus, and who trust the Bible, there is reliable external evidence. For example, for those who affirm that Jesus is God in the flesh, there are His words to the thief on the cross found in Luke 23:43, "...today you will be with me in Paradise." The brain and body of the thief would remain on earth, when he died, but "he" — his soul-person — would continue to live. Affirmation of an immaterial soul-person offers more to gain than there is to lose. In particular, self-distancing, as a function that the soul-person is able to employ, is profoundly strengthened by the simple reality that, "I am more than my brain".

IX.   Arntz and Gitta, *Schema Therapy in Practice: An Introductory Guide to the Schema Mode Approach*, 36-37.

X.   Morgan, *Person and Character Level Life Coaching and Mentoring.*

XI.   Scientific American, "How the Brain Does Attention is Still Unknown".

XII.   Osyerman, Elmore, and Smith, "Self, Self-Concept, and Identity", 69-104.

XIII. Ibid., 72.

XIV.   The *Ten Tasks* are described in Basic 9 in Morgan, *Person and Character Level Life Coaching and Mentoring*, 53-59.

XV.   Bergner and Holmes develop a status dynamic view which, "...maintains that the self-concept is most usefully identified, not with an organized summary of myriad perceived facts about oneself, but with one's summary formulation of one's status. That is to say, it is one's overall conception of one's place or position in relation to all of the elements in one's world, including oneself." Bergner and Holmes, *Self-concepts and Self-concept Change: A Status Dynamic Approach*, 2.

They go on to explain how they work with clients to bring about change to the self-concept.

> In the status dynamic approach to helping persons alter their self-concepts, change is fundamentally about enabling clients to move out of the limiting, self-assigned statuses that are the source of their problems, and assigning themselves new statuses that convey far more behavior potential. To accomplish this objective, the fundamental general strategy of status dynamic therapists is to create a two-person community with their clients, assign certain statuses to them, and treat them with the utmost consistency as persons who have those statuses... Ibid., 5.

The primary means that they use, in other words, to actually achieve this self-concept change is, "...*that of actually placing clients in relational positions that are incompatible with the ones articulated in their self-concepts.*" In *Person and Character Level Life Coaching* terms, this could be understood as contrasting the psychological personality functioning with the character functioning of the soul-person. Ibid., 5.

Bergner and Holmes provide an example, from the therapeutic work of Carl Rogers, of assigning people with a status for their new self-concept:

> ...we see Rogers as someone who assigned to all of his clients the status "unconditionally acceptable human being," not on the basis of observation, but *a priori*. The central element in person-centered therapy, and indeed the element cited by its practitioners as necessary and sufficient by itself to achieve therapeutic change...consisted in providing a relationship in which clients, independently of the facts about their lives and persons, were genuinely regarded and treated as acceptable persons. Ibid., 5.

XVI.   Ibid., 6. Bergner and Holmes assigned a large number of statuses on this same *a priori* basis:

> In status dynamic therapy, the client is regarded and treated, a priori, as a person (1) who is acceptable; (2) who makes sense; (3) whose best interests come first in the therapeutic relationship; (4) who is important and significant to the therapist; (5) who already possesses enabling strengths, knowledge, and other resources for solving problems; (6) who, given a choice between equally realistic but differentially degrading appraisals of him or her, is to be given the benefit of the doubt; and (7) who is an agent (i.e., an individual capable of entertaining behavioral options and selecting from among them, as opposed to a helpless victim of genetic, historical, environmental, or other forces).

XVII.   For a further explanation of these attitudes, please see the Basic 3 chapter in Morgan, *Person and Character Level Life Coaching and Mentoring*, 23-26.

XVIII. Moreland, "Restoring the Substance to the Soul of Psychology", 29-43. Moreland argues that the self is the soul. Morgan, "Soul as the Person Experiencing the Brain's Psychological Functioning". 45-53. Morgan promotes the view that the soul is the person.

XIX.   Thayer's Greek Lexicon, "Spirit — pneuma." At 1 Thessalonians 5:23: "a spirit, i.e. a simple essence, devoid of all or at least all grosser matter, and possessed of the power of knowing, desiring, deciding, and acting.

   a. a life giving spirit
   b. a human soul that has left the body
   c. a spirit higher than man but lower than God, i.e. an angel

       i. used of demons, or evil spirits, who were conceived as inhabiting the bodies of men

      ii. the spiritual nature of Christ, higher than the highest angels and equal to God, the divine nature of Christ"

XX.   Moreland, "Restoring the Substance to the Soul of Psychology", 35-36. According to Moreland,

> The soul also contains various mental states within it, for example, sensations and thoughts. This is not as complicated as it sounds. Water can be in a cold or a hot state. Likewise, the soul can be in a feeling or thinking state. There are at least five different states that can take place within the soul: a sensation, a thought, a belief, a desire, a volition. Now the soul contains more states than these five, but it will be helpful to single these out and explain them more fully. A sensation is a state of awareness or sentience, a mode of consciousness (e.g., a conscious awareness of sound, color, or pain). A thought is a mental content that can be expressed in an entire sentence and that only exists while it is being thought. Some thoughts logically imply other thoughts. For example 'All dogs are mammals' entails 'Some dogs are mammals.' Some thoughts don't entail, but merely provide evidence for, other thoughts. For example, certain thoughts about evidence in a court case provide evidence for the thought that a person is guilty. Finally, a thought exists only while someone is having it, and one can have thoughts that one does not believe. A belief is a person's view accepted to varying degrees of strength, of how things really are. At any given time, one can have many beliefs that are not currently being contemplated. A desire is a certain felt inclination to do, have, avoid, or experience certain things. Desires are either conscious or such that they can be made conscious through certain activities, for example, through therapy. An act of will is a volition, an exercise of power, an endeavoring to do a certain thing.

XXI.   The terms "unregenerate" and "regenerate" are used in their technical theological sense — what it means to be "born again," as referred to in the gospel of John chapter three (John 3:3). The regenerate soul-person has been born again and has, for example, received a new disposition and is freed from the power of sin.

XXII.   Adler, *Intellect: Mind over Matter*. XI. For Adler the intellect covers a number of specific powers. This includes the ability to conceive or understand, the ability to make judgments, and the ability to reason or make inferences. He believes that the exercise of these powers constitutes the range of human thought. He regards the intellect as an immaterial component of human nature, even though it is dependent on brain states and processes. He declares that he is asserting a more limited and qualified type of immaterialism and explains further that:

> It [the limited and qualified immaterialism] asserts that the intellect is an immaterial component of human nature. The intellect cannot normally function without dependence on the activity of the brain, but the brain is not the physical organ of intellectual thought, as the eye together with the brain is the physical organ of vision.

> In other words, of all the powers possessed by human beings, only our intellectual powers and operations are in themselves immaterial. Even though it must be admitted that all the activities of intellectual thought are so dependent on brain states and processes that they cannot occur without them, nevertheless, intellect as such is not reducible to brain, nor are its characteristic activities merely subjective experienced aspects of brain states and processes.

XXIII.   This section borrows heavily from information in Morgan, *Person and Character Level Life Coaching and Mentoring*.

XXIV.   The *Ten Tasks* are described in Basic 9 in Morgan, *Person and Character Level Life Coaching and Mentoring*, 53-59.

XXV.   For a further explanation, please see the Basic 6 chapter in Morgan, *Person and Character Level Life Coaching and Mentoring*, 37-39.

XXVI.   Schwartz, *You Are Not Your Brain: The 4-Step Solution for Changing Bad Habits, Ending Unhealthy Thinking, and Taking Control of Your Life*, 90-91.

XXVII.   For additional information on these shifting psychological parts, please see Basic 5 in Morgan, *Person and Character Level Life Coaching and Mentoring*, 33-36.

XXVIII.Arntz and Gitta, *Schema Therapy in Practice: An Introductory Guide to the Schema Mode Approach*, 36-37.

XXIX. Material in this section is derived from the Book 2 Introduction in Morgan, *Person and Character Level Life Coaching and Mentoring*, 89-99.

XXX. The Values in Action (VIA) Survey of Character Strengths is a simple self-assessment that takes less than 15 minutes and provides a considerable amount of information that is helpful in understanding one's core characteristics. The survey can be taken free of charge at the VIA Institute on Character website: https://www.viacharacter.org/survey/account/register.

REFERENCES

References

Ainsworth, M. D. S. "Attachment Across the Lifespan". *Bulletin of the New York Academy of Medicine*, 61, (1985), 792-812.

Adler, M. *Intellect: Mind over Matter*. New York: Collier Books, 1990.

Alford, B. A. and Beck, A. T. *The Integrative Power of Cognitive Therapy*. New York, NY: Guilford Press, 1998.

Arntz, A. and Gitta J. *Schema Therapy in Practice: An Introductory Guide to the Schema Mode Approach*. Chichester, UK: Wiley-Blackwell, 2013.

Ayduk, O. and Kross, E. "From a Distance: Implications of Spontaneous Self-distancing for Adaptive Self-reflection". *Journal of Personality and Social Psychology*, 98(5), (2010), 809-829.

Beck, R. and McDonald, A. "Attachment to God: The Attachment to God Inventory, Tests of Working Model Correspondence, and an Exploration of Faith Group Differences". *Journal of Psychology and Theology*, 32(2), (2004), 92-103.

Bergner, R. M. and Holmes, J. R. "Self-concepts and Self-concept Change: A Status Dynamic Approach". http://www.sdp.org/sdp/papers/selfconcept.html Accessed 19.December. 2017.

Chalmers, D. J. "Facing up to the Problem of Consciousness". *Journal of Consciousness Studies*, 2 (3), (1995), 200-219.

Cohen, R. I. *Clinical Supervision: What to Do and How to Do It*. Belmont, CA: Brooks/Cole, 2004.

Hubble, M. A., Duncan, B. L., and Miller, S. D. *The Heart & Soul of Change: What Works in Therapy*. Washington, DC: American Psychological Association, 1999.

Kirkpatrick, L. "Attachment and Religious Representations and Behavior". In J. Cassidy & P. R. Shaver (Eds.), *Handbook of Attachment: Theory, Research, and Clinical Applications*. NewYork: Guilford Press, (1999), 803-822.

Klein, S. B. and Gangi, C. E. "The Multiplicity of Self: Neuropsychological Evidence and its Implications for the Self as a Construct in Psychological Research". https://philpapers.org/archive/KLEP-9.pdf Accessed 20.April.2018.

Kross, E. "When the Self Becomes Other: Toward an Integrative Understanding of the Processes Distinguishing Adaptive Self-reflection from Rumination". https://docs.google.com/viewer?url=https%3A%2F%2Fpdfs.semanticscholar.org%2F 06a4%2Fbf87429f8ffb2eb3b94f41d6f9fdd6bcf2ca.pdf Accessed 22.March.2018.

Kross, E., Ayduk, O., and Mischel, W. "When Asking 'Why' Does Not Hurt: Distinguishing Rumination From Reflective Processing of Negative Emotions". Psychological Science, 16(9), (2005), 709-715.

Lawrence, R. T. "Measuring the Image of God: The God Image Inventory and the God Image Scales". *Journal of Psychology and Theology*, 25, (1997), 214-226.

Moreland, J. P. "Restoring the Substance to the Soul of Psychology". *Journal of Psychology and Theology*, 26(1), (1998), 29-43.

Morgan, D. D. *Person and Character Level Life Coaching and Mentoring.* Spillern, Austria: OM EAST, 2017.

Morgan, D. D. "Soul as the Person Experiencing the Brain's Psychological Functioning". *Edification Journal*, 5(1), (2011), 45-53.

Morgan, D. D. *Life in Process.* Wheaton, IL: Victor Books, 1993.

O'Hare, C. *Challenging God Images: Implementing a Christian Component Within a Standard Group Therapy Intervention* (Doctoral dissertation). 2002. Retrieved from ProQuest Dissertations and Theses database. (UMI No. 3062350)

Osyerman, D., Elmore, K., and Smith, G. "Self, Self-Concept, and Identity" in *Handbook of Self and Identity, 2ⁿᵈ Edition*. ed. Leary, M. and Tangney, J. New York: The Guilford Press, 2012.

Rizzuto, A. M. *The Birth of the Living God: A Psychoanalytic Study.* Chicago, IL: University of Chicago Press, 1979.

Schwartz, J. and Gladding, R. *You Are Not Your Brain: The 4-Step Solution for Changing Bad Habits, Ending Unhealthy Thinking, and Taking Control of Your Life.* New York: Avery, 2011.

Scientific American. "How the Brain Does 'Attention' is Still Unknown". https://blogs.scientificamerican.com/guest-blog/how-the-brain-does-attention-is-still-unknown/?print=true Accessed 21.December.2017.

Southwick S. & Charney, D. *Resilience: The Science of Mastering Life's Greatest Challenges.* Cambridge, UK: Cambridge University Press, 2012.

Thayer's Greek Lexicon. In Blue Letter Bible (Version 2.70.1) [Mobile Application Software]. Retrieved from https://www.blueletterbible.org, 2018.

VIA Institute on Character. "The VIA Classification of Character Strengths". https://www.viacharacter.org/www/Character-Strengths Accessed 3.April.2018.